About the Author

Carol Matsumoto (Poquetanuck, CT) had her first paranormal experience when she was four years old and has continued to see spirits throughout her life. She is the owner of the haunted and highly rated bed and breakfast, Captain Grant's, 1754, a national historic inn located in Preston, Connecticut.

Visit her at www.captaingrants.com.

TRUE STORIES FROM A HAUNTED CONNECTICUT INN

THE GHOSTS OF CAPTAIN GRANT'S INN

THE CONNECTICUT PRESS

Madison, CT

The Ghosts of Captain Grant's Inn: True Stories from a Haunted Connecticut Inn © 2017 by Carol Matsumoto. All rights reserved. No part of this book may be used or reproduced in any manner whatsoever, including Internet usage, without written permission from the authors, except in the case of brief quotations embodied in critical articles and reviews.

Revised Edition
2024

Cover design: The Connecticut Press

Photos on pages 12–13, 106, 118, 128, 134, 141, 146, 149 by Bruce Peter Morin; Photos on pages 20, 24, 32, 101 by Carol Matsumoto; Photos on page 192 by Joanna Bagatelle; Photo on page 193 by Rebecca Abrams; Photos on pages 195–196 by Dennis and Carrie Lowe.

The Connecticut Press is a registered trademark of The Connecticut Press, Inc.

Library of Congress Cataloging-in-Publication Data
Names: Matsumoto, Carol, author.
 Title: The ghosts of Captain Grant's Inn : true stories from a haunted Connecticut inn / by Carol Matsumoto.
 Description: Revised Edition. | Madison : The Connecticut Press.
Identifiers: LCCN 2017038689 (print) | LCCN 2017029256 (ebook) | ISBN 9780738754307 (ebook) | ISBN 9780997790788
 Subjects: LCSH: Captain Grant's, 1754 (Inn : Preston, Conn.) | Haunted hotels--Connecticut--Preston. | Ghosts—Connecticut—Preston.
 Classification: LCC BF1474.5 (print) | LCC BF1474.5 .M38 2017 (ebook) | DDC 133.1/297465—dc23
 LC record available at https://lccn.loc.gov/2017038689

All mail addressed to the author is forwarded but the publisher cannot, unless specifically instructed by the author, give out an address or phone number.
 Any Internet references contained in this work are current at publication time, but the publisher cannot guarantee that a specific location will continue to be maintained. Please refer to the publisher's website for links to authors' websites and other sources.

The Connecticut Press
63 West Wharf Road
Madison, CT 06443
https://www.connecticutpress.com

Printed in the United States of America

Dedication

I wish to thank my husband, Tadashi, who assisted me with editing as well as taking on many of my bed and breakfast chores while I sat writing this book. I also want to thank all of the guests who allowed me to use the pictures they had taken.

Contents

Introduction ... 1

Chapter 1: The Past ... 3

Chapter 2: The Purchase ... 11

Chapter 3: The Renovation ... 23

Chapter 4: Ted Number Two ... 35

Chapter 5: New Beginnings ... 45

Chapter 6: Haunted Reality ... 51

Chapter 7: Communicating with Spirits ... 59

Chapter 8: Deborah Adams ... 65

Chapter 9: Daniel ... 75

Chapter 10: Mercy Adelaide Grant ... 81

Chapter 11: Liam ... 87

Chapter 12: Pete ... 95

Chapter 13: The Victim ... 99

Chapter 14: Guest Experiences ... 103

Chapter 15: Adelaide Room ... 105

Chapter 16: Collette Room ... 117

Chapter 17: Elizabeth Room ... 127

Chapter 18: Amy Room ... 133

Chapter 19: Marie Room ... 139

Chapter 20: The Avery Home ... 145

Chapter 21: The Gathering ... 153

Chapter 22: What I've Learned from Spirits ... 163

Chapter 23: Thoughts about Spirits and Communication Methods ... 185

Chapter 24: Cameras and Apparitions ... 191

Chapter 25: Senses ... 201

Conclusion ... 209

Appendix: Spirit Interviews ... 213

INTRODUCTION

This is my story. It is not fiction but an interwoven true story of my struggle to build a business, the saint and spirits that helped me do so, and the supernatural events that led to the path that I would eventually follow. As a story, it has narrative themes that are intertwined but sometimes distinct.

My story begins with the unlikely event of my purchase of an old, dilapidated house built in 1754. The renovations not only became difficult but included uncanny if not miraculous events that continue to happen to this day.

As the business took hold, I learned that twelve spirits occupied the home. As word spread through the media, I began to finally accept the reality of what I had purchased and restored. Little did I know that doors were opening to me thanks to the help of those who had already left this world. Since my business began, I have hosted guests from every continent and from all economic backgrounds and belief systems.

Many of my guests have been ghost hunters searching for the world beyond their grasp. They bring their equipment and hope to experience new phenomena. Most are young and this is their current fad. Others are quite serious and hope to prove the existence of life after death.

One day a family arrived for a visit that opened my mind and changed my belief system forever. I learned that I had the ability to communicate with the spirit world. That journey has not ended. It has brought me to conclusions about the afterlife that are detailed in the last half of this book. Where are we headed? Where have we been? What does faith have to do with all of this?

This is only the beginning of the journey. The spirits continue to occupy the home. They entertain our guests, but they are not in charge. There is a higher power that dictates what happens to them, just as it dictates what happens to us.

Chapter 1
THE PAST

I was born in Grafton, North Dakota, in 1945. I was like every other child brought up in the forties and fifties. Well, almost. I had my first encounter with the paranormal when I was four years old. My sister Roberta was an infant, so that is how I remember my exact age. My family was traveling home from Fargo, headed to Grand Forks and on to Minto, where we lived. It was dark outside, and in North Dakota in 1949 there would not have been any road lights for the sixty-some miles of the trip, only the headlights of my dad's car. There are barely any road lights there today.

We traveled on old Route 81 going north. Five miles or so out of Fargo, a large red ball of fire came down from the sky and followed my dad's car until we saw the lights of Grand Forks. This ball of fire terrified my mother but did not scare me at all. I clearly remember thinking, "They are not going to hurt us." But I was only four years old and had to follow my parents' orders to lie down in the back seat of our car. The seat material was gray and made of wool and I remember how scratchy it was. I continued to lie there, and all I felt was curiosity. I wanted to see what was going on, but every time I tried to get up my mother screamed, "Lie down!" She was hysterical. She kept telling me to lie as flat as I could on the car seat and kept ordering my father to do something. "Go faster! Go slower!" she would cry. He kept saying, "It goes faster if I step on the gas, so I am just going to go at a steady fifty-five and see what happens."

Nothing worked. Whatever it was, it came up alongside of us in the ditch on the right-hand side by my mother. The ditches along the main roads in North Dakota are wide and deep. They help drain the floodwaters off the roads during snow melt and heavy rains that arrive nearly every year in the spring. The red ball of fire, or maybe flickering red light, filled the ditch from end to end. When my father saw the lights of the city of Grand Forks, the entity rose. It shot into the sky above us and headed north.

The following day, my dad warned my mother and me that we were never to mention the incident again. He said we would not be believed and everyone in town would think we were crazy. We obeyed that order to be silent for over thirty-five years. In my forties, and already a resident of Connecticut, I decided to drive my dad out east. In my kitchen, in Preston, I got the courage to ask him about that night. "Dad, do you remember the night that the red ball of fire followed us from Fargo to Grand Forks?" He stared at me, shook his head, and said, "I can't believe you still remember that."

What I didn't tell my father was about the experiences I had following that nighttime adventure. When I was about twelve years old, I had a terrifying experience. My day had started out like any other. It was summer, so I slept until nine and got up for breakfast. I remember getting a call from my friend Marge, but after that I couldn't recall anything. There was about a four-hour time lapse. I was in my bedroom, but I didn't know how I had gotten there or where I had been before. My back was against the bedroom wall and I was so scared I couldn't breathe. I looked apprehensively out my bedroom window. There was no one around, no one home. Just me. "What happened to me?" I thought. "Where have I been?" I knew I had to escape, but where would I go? I felt that my life was in peril. "There is no one to protect me," I thought. I made the decision to run through the dining room and then the kitchen and down the back staircase. I have never been so scared in my entire life. I told no one about this. Later, my mother asked where I had been all morning and I said, "Out."

From that time on, paranormal experiences followed me wherever I lived. As a child, I could hear soldiers coming up the stairs, but they never arrived. I knew things before I had been informed of them. This didn't go over well at home, and my mother said that I scared her. "You're just like your aunt Bishoi," she would say. Bishoi was my aunt Bernice. I loved her, and this also didn't help the situation at home. My mother was always jealous of her sister. My aunt Bernice had mental health problems throughout her life, but I have often wondered who or what created them.

I was having ongoing paranormal experiences, but I had no idea what they were or what was causing them. I had no knowledge of spirits, souls, aliens, or anything else.

By the time I graduated from high school and left for college, I knew that I would never return to Minto. My dad loved me, but he had to contend with my mother and that is where the break came. My mother simply could not cope with me. She was more scared of my abilities and was glad that I was old enough to be on my own. I remained somewhat close to my dad. He was the parent who told me that I had it in me to accomplish anything. Soon I was to turn eighteen.

Although I entered college, there was no way for me to support my education and myself. I made the decision to marry right out of high school. I moved with my new husband, Ted, to East Grand Forks, Minnesota, where we lived for almost three years. My contacts with my family in Minto were minimal.

But I was no longer alone, as my grandmother Blanche lived in Grand Forks and was always there to encourage me. We had become very close, seeing each other often. She meant a great deal to me and gave me much love and guidance. After three years of marriage, I was pregnant with my second child. I had picked out two names, Emery and Leonard. I decided to call my grandmother and tell her the names I had chosen in case the baby was a boy. When I said the names, she gasped. "Where did you get the idea for those names?" she said. I replied that I had always liked them. Then all I heard was heavy breathing. Finally she asked me to come and see her and said that my aunt Delphine would be there with her.

I arrived on her doorstep completely at a loss. She escorted me into the kitchen, and there she told me about my family. I was told the secrets that no one else of my generation knew. One interesting fact was that I had two uncles that no one in the family knew about, including my aunts and uncles who were their brothers and sisters. These uncles were named Emery and Leonard. They had been born without help from anyone, midwife or doctor. They had both been oxygen-deprived and suffered deep repercussions. In their first year of life they were admitted to an institution for the retarded and remained there throughout their lives. My aunts and uncles didn't find out about them until my grandmother died. Her will revealed all.

My grandmother and I talked for hours. I was amazed at the information she gave me. Now my life began to make sense. I wasn't just an unusual member in a slightly unusual family. We were either very intelligent or at the other end of the intellectual spectrum.

In 1967 my husband and I moved to St. Paul, Minnesota, and within the year purchased our first home in Coon Rapids, just north of Minneapolis. The house was seriously haunted and was the first place where a spirit materialized in front of me. I had gone to bed and was sitting up waiting for my husband, who was having a glass of water in the kitchen. Suddenly a round mist appeared on top of our chest of drawers. It quickly grew legs and then arms. I just sat there totally stunned. Then I called for my husband and the mist disappeared, arms going first, legs next, and lastly the head. I believe the spirit was the husband of the woman from whom we had purchased the house. He had died the year before in a motorcycle accident.

It was also in this neighborhood that we built a new home and then a second home. The second home had mysterious happenings on an ongoing basis. Wind would tear around the house but nowhere else in the neighborhood. When we purchased the land, we uncovered a round circle of stones that would have been in a stream bed at one time. The land had not been cleared since the time of Indian ownership, so no "white" man had created the circle. I often wondered about that stone circle and the troubles that we had in the house. I would occasionally hear a man call out my name in a loud voice. No one was ever there. Nothing else was ever said.

The most mysterious event happened in the early eighties. My husband and I were woken by a terrible storm with high winds. It lasted for over an hour. In the morning three trees had been uprooted. One of them lay on our second-floor deck. That morning I went to a coffee clutch with my neighbors. They talked about their children but no one mentioned the storm. I said, "Wasn't that an awful storm last night?" They all looked at me as if I were from another planet. We were the only house on the block that had experienced a storm.

I talked to my neighbor across the street from us about the storm and she said, "Follow me." She marched back to my house and went up the stairs and down the hall. Then she opened the closet door. (Mind you, this woman had never been in my house.) She started pulling things off the floor, and there, unbeknownst to me, was a Ouija board. She grabbed the board, marched back across the street, went into her living room, took some matches, broke the board into sections, and then set it on fire in her fireplace. When I asked her how she knew the board was there, her only answer was, "I don't know. I just knew." I had no idea that we owned a Ouija board. My daughter had bought the board but had never mentioned it to me. That was the end of our individual storms.

While in Coon Rapids I returned to college and soon after was divorced. I decided to apply to colleges around the country for a graduate degree and ended up in Connecticut in another haunted house.

This is where I first captured spirits on film with my camera. I first took a picture of a spirit when I moved into the home I now live in. It looked like energy somewhat in the shape of a man walking. I took the picture on a sunny afternoon in August. I hadn't moved into the home yet and was there to see what I could expect of the house at the closing. When I saw the picture after the film had been developed, I thought that either the film was bad or something had gone wrong with the camera.

That Christmas, four months later, I took another picture of the same area. There he was again. It was 10:00 p.m. The only light was from lamps and a flash on the camera—no bright sunlight streaming through the windows. His arms were outstretched and his legs were apart, and he looked like he wanted to go into the house. It was just like the summer picture taken in the sunlight. That's when I knew I had a ghost on film. I call him "the ghost at the original back door." I refer to him by that name because the original house dates to 1790. In 1827 a new addition was built onto the back of the house, moving the back door twenty feet further away.

Here I lived with a man for six years. I was desperately unhappy being in a job I didn't want and a relationship that was not good for either of us. I decided to end the affair and then began to pray for guidance. I had made some pretty serious mistakes in my life, and any shove in the right direction couldn't hurt. I had also been reading the Bible for quite some time.

After a year of being alone, I began to ask St. Anthony to help me find a home that I could make into a bed and breakfast. St. Anthony is the saint of lost things. Once a month for one year I got a small windfall of money from a source that I didn't know existed: a forgotten insurance policy, an abandoned bank account, etc. In the month of May, someone made my mortgage payment for me. I took the money I received and put it in a savings account. I called it my money account for a new start.

At the end of one year I had over $16,000, a real windfall. I knew that I needed to invest the money, but where? I went to North Carolina to visit an aunt and uncle, and while there I investigated opening a bed and breakfast. The restrictions were too cumbersome and I returned home. I mentioned my idea to friends and family. No one liked my idea. Bad, bad, bad was all I heard. That is when I first got the feeling that my future lay right next door.

Now for my story.

Chapter 2
THE PURCHASE

I own Captain Grant's Inn, a bed and breakfast in Poquetanuck, Connecticut. Poquetanuck is a small historic village within the town of Preston in southeastern Connecticut. The home I call Captain Grant's was built in 1754 and the village it is in dates back to 1687. Behind Captain Grant's is a cemetery dating to the mid-1600s. Across the street is the new cemetery dating to the early 1800s. I tell guests that I have more dead neighbors than live ones.

The name of the inn comes from Captain William Avery Gonzales Grant, who lived in the home with his wife, Mercy Adelaide Grant, and two children. Captain Grant died at sea off Cape Hatteras when he was thirty-two years old. Mercy was pregnant with their third child. Although Mercy died in the 1800s, she continues to occupy the home, as does one of her children. She says that she is still waiting for the captain to return.

Captain Grant's after its extensive restoration.
Photo credit: Bruce Peter Morin

The cemetery behind Captain Grant's dates back to the mid-1600s.
Photo credit: Bruce Peter Morin

The newer cemetery across the street from Captain Grant's dates back to the early 1800s. Photo credit: Bruce Peter Morin

The Avery home, located next door to Captain Grant's, is the first house the author purchased in Connecticut. Photo credit: Bruce Peter Morin

In 1993 I lived in the home next door to Captain Grant's, the Avery home, and I would look up at the house every time I did the dishes. It sits high on a hill. I would think, "What a stately home it is." At night I would look up at the attic windows from my bedroom and look for ghosts to appear. I'm sorry to say that I never saw one. I could almost imagine what it would look like: a dark figure standing in the window looking out at the world.

My imagination also had me thinking about my retirement. When I was forty-eight years old, I decided that I didn't want to retire on only Social Security. When I was divorced I lost my IRA and did not see many opportunities for additional income unless I remarried, and marriage at that time was out of the question. I wanted to be in charge of my own life. One day, while I was looking out my kitchen window, I had the idea that I should buy the neighboring house and make it into a bed and breakfast. Then I would have a decent income in my old age, with no worry about living on Social Security. Dreams are usually better than reality, but this time the reality became far better than the dream. An awesome journey now lay ahead of me.

The old structure had been on the market for two years and I decided to make an offer. I phoned the real estate agent and learned that the current tenants also wanted to purchase the home. I told the agent that I still wanted to see the home, especially the interior. She told me that it would take the tenants at least a week to clear a path through the house. She set up a time for me to see the inside eight days later. As soon as I entered the back door I saw the condition of the interior. It was beyond messy. Trash was everywhere. The floor was littered and the furniture was covered with all kinds of stuff, but there was a path. I thought to myself, "The inside is worse than the outside, and the outside is awful." In the summer the tenants cut their grass three times. That was three times total all summer. Garbage was thrown outside into an area that had a lot of tree saplings. I considered the overall situation and decided to mull it over and make a decision that night. I told the real estate agent that I would call her the next day.

That night I thought about the tenants next door. Seeing how they maintained the place, I could see that having them as next-door neighbors would reduce the value of the home that I was currently living in. If I ever wanted to move, it would be very hard to sell my home. Then there was the cost of the house next door. It started out at $149,000 but had been reduced to $89,900. I still couldn't afford it, but the price was tantalizingly close.

I called the real estate agent the following morning and told her of my intent to make an offer. I told her I could afford to pay $70,000. She told me that the current tenants had made a bid of $84,000. "But," she said "they want the owner to carry the mortgage." That was good news.

The next day the real estate agent phoned to give me the owner's response. He was angry with the current residents for trashing his home and the property. He said that if I increased my bid by $4,000 he would sell the house to me. I agreed and was now about to own the home for half of the original asking price.

I told the agent that I wouldn't go to the closing until the current tenants had moved out. I didn't want expensive attorney fees or a fight in court to get them evicted. I had been told by the agent that they refused to move and had stopped paying rent. It was now November. Winter was a time of year when the tenants could fight eviction due to having children. It didn't matter if they paid rent or not. The owner finally agreed to find them a new rental. He let me know that it had cost him $6,000 to get them out. It took three months and then they were gone.

Finally, on Friday, February 13, 1994, I became the proud owner of a falling-down wreck of a house. Little did I know that there were twelve spirits in residence. At the closing, my attorney stood up before I signed the papers and said, "I need to tell you that you are going to fail." Then he sat down. I was mortified that he would say such a thing. I looked at him, my mouth open, and then signed my way into a new life. Next, I fired my attorney.

Now I had a costly renovation in front of me and only $112 left in the bank. As a single woman, what was I to do next? I prayed every day and decided to take some time and kneel. I asked for a lot of material things back then. I needed immediate help to get the renovations started. On a late-night whim, I decided to ask for a new husband. Maybe God would send me one. He would have to be hardworking and smart and have similar values. Then I went to sleep. I had no idea that the spirits in the Grant home were also working for me.

It was at this time that I decided to see a psychic. She told me that I was going to marry Ted in 1996. I said, "Been there, done that." No way was I going back. She also told me that when I met the right man, he would have a hill across the street from him, with houses on the top of the hill. She said that the house on the left looking up at the hill would be painted green, not a common color for a house. I wrote down what she said, put the script in my attic, and didn't read it again for a year.

The following day, after the closing, I phoned my aunt Shirley in Minnesota to ask her if I should call my ex-husband for help. I often asked for her advice. My former husband was a master carpenter and had all the skills I needed to get the renovations done. We hadn't spoken in thirteen years and the divorce had been a bit nasty, which is all too common. My aunt said, "Carol Jean, are you crazy? No, I don't think you should call him." She never got hysterical, but her voice was a bit faster and higher in response to this question. We talked a bit more and then hung up.

Five minutes later Shirley called back. "Arch says you should call him." Arch is Shirley's husband and my uncle.

"Okay, but why?" I asked.

"Arch says, what do you have to lose? You live 1,500 miles apart. If your ex-husband doesn't want to help you, he's not going to stop by and give you a hard time." Again I hung up, but this time I stared at the phone.

I was sure that St. Anthony had helped me get the house, so I knelt down and prayed. I asked him to intervene with Christ and protect me when I made the call. First I needed to ask one of my children to give me my ex's phone number. My daughter was reluctant but eventually relented and gave me her dad's number. She thought I might make him angry. I really didn't know because she and I rarely talked about him. I summoned all of my courage and then made the call.

"Hi." There was that oh-so-familiar voice.

"Hi, it's Carol. Could we talk for a few minutes?" As I write this, I feel myself shake, as if this occurred only yesterday and not twenty years ago.

"I've been waiting for your call." He didn't explain and I didn't ask. One thing I knew was that he had his life now and I had mine. If he wanted to share something with me, it was his choice. When we divorced, he had paid only one child support check, so he owed me about $30,000.

"I have a proposal for you," I said. "I bought a house and I want to make it into a bed and breakfast, but it needs a lot of work. If you would help me out, I will go to court and lift the court judgment against you." Years earlier, the state of Minnesota had put a judgment against him for not paying child support. I took a deep breath and held it while waiting for his answer. I was so tense that if I had bent, I would have broken in two.

His response was startling. "I had a dream a couple of nights ago. Christ spoke to me and told me that you would call. He said that I should do what you ask. I'm packed and the gang box is packed as well, but I have a problem. I'm laid off and don't have enough money to make the trip."

Was he lying or telling the truth? He had seldom ever lied to me. There was no way for me to know. He wasn't a religious person when we were married. "He must have gone through some spiritual changes," I thought.

I considered this for a couple of seconds. "How much do you need?"

"About $400 for gas and food. I'll drive straight through so there won't be any hotel costs."

Maybe I was naive, but I said to my ex, "I will have to wait until my next paycheck and then I'll send you the money."

We talked for a few more minutes and then hung up. I immediately called Shirley. "He's coming."

She responded in a gasping voice, "He is? Well I guess Arch was right."

Then I called my daughter and son, who by now had their own homes and careers, to let them know that their dad was coming to Connecticut and would be here in about two weeks. Their relationship with their dad was ongoing but at a distance, since they lived in Connecticut near me and he lived in Minnesota. Now, all of our lives were about to change.

When Ted arrived, I had him stay in the bed and breakfast, which we called "the big house," for the next nine months. I had not sold the home I lived in (the Avery house), so I continued to stay there. Ted's bedroom was the largest room in the big house. It took about two days for him to say to me, "The house is haunted." This wasn't entirely a surprise to me. He also told me about nightly visits from an entity, but he didn't ask to move to another room. When I asked him questions, he would mumble something and then change the subject. He did mention something about a religious picture that would end up on the floor upside down on its own, but not much else. Considering our estrangement, I wasn't about to pry.

Our first project was to clean out the house. I had asked for the use of a thirteen-yard dumpster to be included in the house closing, and we began to fill it. Then we filled Ted's large pickup truck an additional nine times. Ceilings were torn down, inside walls were moved, and holes were drilled into two large beams. Cables were run through the holes, drawing the west outer wall back into place. It was close to falling into the yard.

While working on projects inside the house, we would often hear sounds coming from the second floor but did not think much of it at the time. We knew the house was haunted, but there was too much work to do to think seriously about it. It never scared me. I believe that I instinctively knew the spirits were friendly. What I didn't know at that time was that they were pulling for me to finish the house. During the renovations I made every attempt to restore the house to its original character. I think that the spirits who lived there wanted exactly that. I often said to myself that if I followed the right path, the universe would open up before me.

By April much work had been done to the inside of the house, and it was now warm enough to get started cleaning and excavating the outside.

This is a photo of Captain Grant's yard in April 1994 after the garbage was removed but before the brush was cut back and burned. Photo credit: author

Behind the home there were bedsprings standing on end in the lawn. They had been frozen into the ground during the winter. Then there were the unwanted tree saplings and the outside garbage. I made a fire pit behind the house and started burning brush. I burned every day for eight weeks. Ted removed the garbage and started to take down the asbestos shakes that were on the house. I wanted to expose the original clapboard siding to be more authentic to the period of the house. We easily filled two large wooden boxes that had been left on the property. Once filled, the boxes were taken to the town dump.

When we did this, there were no laws about asbestos siding removal. Just the same, a week later a Connecticut state trooper knocked on my door. "I've been watching you remove the siding," he said.

"Uh huh. Yes, sir," I said.

Then he asked me, "Where did it go?"

I explained that it was sealed in wooden boxes and taken to the dump.

"Does the dump know what was in those boxes?" asked the trooper.

Ted stepped in and said, "Yes, they do. I told them."

"I'll be back," said the trooper. "I'm going to take a ride to the dump." And off he went to the Preston town dump.

About a half hour later the trooper returned and told us that he warned the town not to take any more asbestos and that I wouldn't be fined. I was relieved. Another hurdle crossed. Two weeks later the state enacted asbestos-removal laws. I had just made the deadline on that one.

April was a very busy month. Not only did the siding get taken away and the brush and small trees get burned, but I got my license to operate a bed and breakfast. The next thing that happened was a bit of a disaster. The back cellar wall collapsed, dropping the house eight inches in one corner.

The license from the state was an easy thing to get. All I had to do was go through zoning and get a permit. At that time the town of Preston allowed only two bedrooms in a bed and breakfast. I thought, "That's okay to start. I'll go back later and ask for more rooms." I was so naive. Preston was an old farming community run by men according to their agricultural norms for society. In 1994 men did the hard outside work and women tended to the cooking and the children. Men ruled and women listened.

When I faced the zoning board to ask for my permit, I was shocked to see only men who couldn't possibly comprehend what I was asking for. They didn't, but it didn't matter. They were dubious, to say the least, that I could pull this off. At that time there was only one small bed and breakfast in town to act as a reference for what the town should expect from me.

One of the men asked me for clarification. "You're talking about the old Congdon home?" I said yes and they started to chuckle. Someone laughed out loud. They told me that some reputable engineers and construction companies had looked at the home and decided it was beyond repair. I told them that I was in front of the zoning board to get my permit to operate a bed and breakfast and that I would have a building permit for every part of the renovation.

They immediately voted and I got my license. They never believed that I would get it done, but no one knew the spirits were rooting for me—including me.

Chapter 3
THE RENOVATION

Throughout the initial fifteen months of renovations, amazing things happened. When I needed something, it would be made available to me. I now know that I had a lot of help from St. Anthony and the spirits in the house. This continues to this day, but on a smaller scale. I needed a lot of help from them in 1994. Here are a few things that happened.

The back cellar wall was a bit problematic. It collapsed within two months of buying the house. It happened while I was at work. When I got home, the yard was covered in stone. Ted had pulled all of the stone out of the cellar with his pickup, and now there it sat on my lawn. I went into the house and looked at the dining room floor. It was at an eight-inch slant. "Rats," I said, while thinking out loud. "What do we do with that?" Ted asked for money to purchase house supports and I went to my room to beseech St. Anthony one more time.

In 1754 homes were built with dry stone foundations. No mortar was used. They would dig a hole and lay stone around the perimeter, and when they couldn't lift the stone high enough anymore, they would fill the cellar with dirt and continue laying stones until they reached the desired height. When they were done, they would dig the dirt back out of the cellar. Houses such as Captain Grant's also have a 6' x 8' center foundation to help hold the house up. There are beams crossing the ceilings in two separate directions. Where they meet there is a large post. All of this makes the house very heavy. The walls are slightly tilted inward so that the weight of the home is supported on the center stone structure as well as the exterior wall. All of this helped keep the home from collapsing.

In March 1994 the yard was full of the stones that once formed the back cellar of Captain Grant's. Photo credit: author

I went to work the next day and Ted got house supports to keep the house from falling more than it already had. They didn't work. I came home that night and he told me that the supports were breaking. The house was just too heavy for ordinary house jacks. He had been asking around about where to find commercial staging. "Providence, Rhode Island, is the only place I found that carries what we need," he said. He also told me that the rental was $600 a month.

"Okay," I answered. "Can you get this done in one month?" He said yes and off to Providence we went.

I got the permit for the cellar wall, rebar went in, and Ted ordered the cement block and set up a time for the cement pour. He called the town inspector and told him the date and time for the cement delivery.

The inspector never arrived. After an hour Ted told me to get my camera and start shooting pictures because we had to do the pour. Well, the pour went smoothly, the cement blocks went up, and the inspector approved my pictures. Without Ted there to help me, the project that cost me $1,000 would have cost $12,000.

Ted did not mention the spirits again, and I was too busy to notice if anything paranormal was happening. Once in a while I would go into the attic and talk to the spirits. The air was heavy and I knew they were there, but I still didn't know how to communicate with them. But after a series of uncanny coincidences, everything was falling into place. I knew without a doubt that I was being helped from beyond this world.

Work continued almost every day. All of the windows were reset, caulked, and reinstalled. The hallway on the second floor was lengthened and a door to what was going to be a second-floor deck was added. Oak was purchased from a saw mill and a foundation for a 10' x 30' deck was going in. When I purchased the oak, I carried it home in my Acura hatchback board by board. I was a determined woman.

In the early 1900s two sisters had inherited the home. One was getting married and the other sister slept with her sister's intended husband. A life of mutual hatred began, and it was focused on the house. They tried to cut the structure in half. They put in two front and back doors and cut a channel through the house. A wall was set into this channel. It was now impossible to get from one side of the house to the other without going outside. The house was still that way when I purchased it. It was now time for a door to be put in the kitchen wall, opening up the two sides of the house.

It was a miracle in the first place that I even got the house at the price I paid, but now in the throes of renovations miracles or coincidences were happening on a weekly basis. Ted had taken down the ceiling in the east kitchen (each sister had a kitchen) and found that a previous owner had cut through a support beam in order to get plumbing to the second floor. There was a 600-pound tub sitting just above this break in the beam. Ted told me that I was lucky the tub hadn't gone clear through to the basement.

We weren't able to lift the tub, so demolition became the method of choice. Even small sections of the tub were heavy. Finally it was removed and the job of replacing the cut beam became primary. What was needed was a six-inch-wide laminated beam. Ted had gone to the lumberyard and was told that what we needed cost $24.95 per running foot. I needed at least seventeen feet. Then he asked me what I wanted to do. I told him that I was going to go and pray, and I did just that. I didn't know if St. Anthony could help with this one, but I was going to pray anyway.

That night, on the way to work the next day, and on the way home, I prayed. And then it was the evening of the next day. When I returned home, Ted told me that he had gone to the dump that day. When he got in line, there was a construction truck in front of him. On that truck was a long laminated beam. He asked the driver how long the beam was. It was a healthy eighteen feet. Then he asked if he could have it. "Thank you." The universe had just helped me again!

Fall was on the way, with winter not far behind. The house had no insulation. The outside walls of the home had posts and beams. Between the posts were wide boards of wood. The outside siding was nailed to the wood. Inside they had attached lath to the wood and plastered over that. That left no inner wall for insulation. The walls were cold and wind blew through the windows. Ted had an idea for how to insulate: put up 2 x 3s on the inside of the existing walls, insulate, and then sheetrock. "Great idea," I thought. We went forward and I bought the lumber that was needed for the new inside walls. Now, Ted was ready to install sheetrock. More money was needed. I thought, "I won't eat next week. That will give me some money."

It was Sunday morning and I was at the big house talking with Ted about the sheetrock. We had the radio on, tuned to a Norwich station. For fifteen minutes on Sunday morning they had a program called "Swap and Sell." I had it on but was not listening very closely. Then a women spoke up and said she was from Preston and had twelve sheets of 4' x 12' sheetrock to give away. I listened, then took her number and called her immediately. I told her that I was Carol Collette and I was restoring the old Congdon home. She told me that she admired what I was doing and would save the sheetrock for me. So it turned out that I did not have to purchase any more sheetrock for the first floor. Another amazing coincidence! Thank you, God.

The guys at the dump started to save things for me. I got eighteenth-century doors complete with hardware, wagons for hauling stuff around, bedsprings, and all in all about $12,000 worth of building materials for the initial renovation. If it was old, they saved it for me to look at. I can't say enough about how wonderful those guys at the dump were.

One day I got a call from the first selectman (mayor to most). He said, "They're tearing down a home on Route 165 near Fleming's Feed and Seed. It's eighteenth century. They have some old siding set aside for you. Do you need it?" When Ted had removed the asbestos shakes, there were several runs of ruined siding underneath.

I was also informed that the zoning board had talked about the house at their last meeting and they had a suggestion for me. "Yes," I said hesitantly. "What is it?"

"We would like you to paint the house the same color that it was in the 1700s."

They couldn't order me to comply with their color choice, but I was flattered that they had noticed the house was coming along. After restoring the siding with what they had given me, I began to paint the outside and decided to go with light yellow siding and dark green trim. This was just what they wanted. I figured it was a good idea to have a happy zoning board.

Now that the painting was done, I began to think about having a walkway to the front door. Ted had a suggestion. All that stone from the basement wall would be perfect for the job. We would use the stone for a front walkway. I agreed. He also wanted to contour the front yard so that the incline was less steep. "Great idea," I replied, while thinking of how much work this would entail. Well, it turned out to be one of the most difficult jobs I have ever done.

I rented a front end loader. Ted did the contouring of the lawn. Then my son, Glen, came to help. He lifted the heavy stones from the backyard with the front end loader and placed them on what was becoming the new walkway. Once that was done, my daughter, Holly, helped me put in the smaller stones. Some of these smaller stones weighed well over two hundred pounds. It's amazing what a person can do when they put their mind to it!

When the walkway was finally done, I started to build a retaining wall to hold up the soil that had been pushed against the house. By the end of the job I had lost twenty pounds.

It was now time for the interior work to begin. I did all of the painting. I scraped and sanded the original bedroom floors by hand. My son would come over after work and help by sanding the first-level floors and hooking up plumbing in the kitchen. I had purchased some cheap wood paneling and had Ted cut it to fit between the ceiling beams before he left. That autumn, Ted returned to Minnesota. He had reestablished a relationship with his adult children, Glen and Holly, and Ted and I departed friends. It was truly a healing experience for all of us.

The first thing I did was clean the beams. Ted had tried sand blasting. The wood was so hard that nothing happened except a large mess ended up on the floor. My next attempt was to make a mixture of Murphy's Oil Soap, bleach, and water and start to scrub, using old towels for rags. It worked like a charm. By now I had muscles like a man. I was a real he-woman!

I bought Williamsburg Whitewash and painted the paneling strips that Ted had cut into a thick crosshatch pattern. The thick paint stood up on the surface and gave the boards a three-dimensional look. Once they were dry, my daughter came over and together we hung the boards between the beams with a nail gun that I had purchased. The beams had all been cleaned and stained an even color ahead of time. Over the course of the winter, the home took on a look of completion. I was beginning to think about opening my doors to the public. By now I was talking to the spirits on a daily basis. I really had no idea if they were listening to me—but they were.

In late spring of that year, my father died. I immediately flew out to North Dakota to be with my mother and three sisters. My father was eighty-four years old at the time of his passing. He was very close to my mother and my sister Brenda, who lived at home. Shortly after he died, they saw him come through the front door of their apartment. They were watching television at the time. Although startled, my mother had the wherewithal to ask him what he was doing there. They both heard him answer, "I'm here to shave." With that, he walked into the bathroom and vanished. My mother was afraid that she wouldn't be believed, but I believed every word of what she said. I had seen my own spirits and I knew they existed. After five days I returned home to Connecticut.

It is said that God acts in mysterious ways. We don't always know that a hardship may be a path to where we need to be. After returning from my sojourn in North Dakota, I was told that I was on a two-week suspension due to being depressed about my father. I was not depressed. I knew it and they knew it. I was in a leadership position and knew enough about the company to know that something was coming down the pike.

After I returned to work after my two-week suspension for being "depressed," I was taken out to lunch by my supervisor. I was questioned about what had happened at work while I was gone. An employee had brought her child to work and let her sleep overnight. The employee said that I had given her permission. Even though none of this might have happened, it gave them an excuse to fire me. Now I felt depressed. I was told that if I wanted to get unemployment, I needed to work two more weeks and keep my mouth shut. I did just that and then they fought unemployment anyway.

After applying for unemployment benefits, I received a call from the unemployment office telling me that I had been turned down and would receive nothing. I burst into tears and raged against God. I was not at home at the time. I cried all the way back home in my car. How could I make it with the bed and breakfast? It still wasn't open. After getting fired, it would be very hard to find other employment. My mind raced. What would I do?

When I pulled into the driveway I had finally stopped sobbing. My eyes were red and puffy and I looked like hell. I went into the house and noticed the answering machine light blinking. "Is that more bad news?" I wondered. I hit the button on the machine to listen to the recording.

"Hello. This is State Unemployment. We need to apologize. When we spoke to you earlier we told you that you were denied unemployment. That is incorrect. You will be getting unemployment for up to one year. Call us to verify that you got this message."

Well, I wasn't done sobbing. I spent the next minutes apologizing to God and thanking him over and over again. I wouldn't lose the big house. Another unexpected turn of good fortune! Thank you.

I now had to try to find a new job, but I didn't have to settle for less pay to keep my unemployment. That was an advantage since I had received a decent salary at my last job. I also had to open the doors of the bed and breakfast soon. I had four weeks of severance pay, and if I could work my buns off, I could start to rent out rooms. I called my aunt Shirley and she agreed to fly out. I bought used furniture and took whatever I was living with and got the home furnished. Two weeks after being fired, I opened my doors to the public—all two rooms.

It was Memorial Day weekend of 1995 and the big house officially became "Captain Grant's, 1754." I was in business. My first four guests stayed, had breakfast, and left. I was ecstatic. I was making a few dollars on my own, but it wasn't enough to sustain me. I needed another job or more rooms.

I had been applying for jobs. I finally took a freelance job with an insurance company. I was to assess individuals that had AIDS and determine if they could work or not. After two weeks I couldn't stand it any longer. The job was really to determine that, no matter how sick they were, they were able to work. My last interview was with a man who was clearly dying. When I sent in my report, I received a call telling me that was not what I was supposed to determine. I told them that there was no way the man could work. That was it—the end of freelancing for an insurance company.

I applied for jobs every week. There was no Internet at that time and job hunting meant sending out resumes, having interviews, being turned down, and feeling anxious about having no money. Every day that I was out looking for work meant nothing was getting done on the bed and breakfast.

The 1952 Buick Roadmaster that proved to be very lucky and profitable for me. Photo credit: author

I happened to have a 1952 Buick Roadmaster. It was an asset that I decided I didn't need to have. On a Friday I drove the car onto the front lawn of the bed and breakfast and put a large "for sale" sign on it. Shortly thereafter, Ted called from Minnesota and asked if he could renovate the two front bedrooms in exchange for the car. I had mentioned to him before he left that I wanted to sell the car. I was ecstatic.

"Absolutely!" I said. Then the "for sale" sign came down. I left the car on the lawn just in case he decided not to take it.

Ted returned from Minnesota in less than a week and immediately began working. Two bathrooms had to go into the two bedrooms that were situated in the front of the house on the second floor. With not enough inner wall space, we had to get creative. We decided to create a channel going up the wall for a plumbing route. This channel looked exactly like a covered post. It worked perfectly. Two more bedrooms were in the making.

Chapter 4
TED NUMBER TWO

I was dating at that time, although not steadily. I decided that a night out on occasion would help me keep my sanity. All work and no play is not a good thing.

In July I received a call from a man wanting to play poker at Foxwoods Casino. He requested a room for Saturday night. I was enchanted by his voice, so deep and soothing. I said nothing to him about that, feeling a little foolish on the phone. When he arrived I checked him into his room. He touched my face and then backed away. I didn't back away but just stood there and smiled, a strange reaction for me. He was different somehow. Trustworthy maybe.

Well, he (his name was also Ted, but I am going to call him by his given name, Tadashi—my children came to call him "Ted number two") came every weekend and then in August asked me to go to the casino with him. I had put $20 in a slot machine on two occasions in the past but otherwise knew nothing of casinos and gambling. Tadashi had been playing poker during the day and was down $300. While just making conversation, he asked me if I could win it back for him at the blackjack table. I explained to him that I had never played blackjack. That did not seem to matter. He handed me $100 and off to a $5 table we went. I was given a couple of lessons and then we started to play. I just kept winning and within a half hour had won back all of Tadashi's money. We had dinner and then he drove me back to Captain Grant's. I had to get up early to make breakfast for my guests in the morning.

The following weekend Tadashi came back to stay and again asked me out. I had the same luck at the blackjack table again, winning about $300. The gambling was making me quite nervous. I loved penny ante poker, but $5 bets were way above my comfort level. It didn't seem to matter to Tadashi.

The following weekend Tadashi left on vacation with someone else he had been seeing. He said he would call me when he got back, but that didn't happen. Instead he waited two weeks and then called. He wasn't certain that he wanted to see me again. I thought, "Then why are you calling me? Of course you want to see me."

At the end of the conversation he told me that he had business in Hartford in two weeks and would come to Captain Grant's after the business was completed. "Do you have a room?" he asked. Of course I had a room. This man was so infuriating, but I liked him too much to say no.

On Sunday after breakfast he asked me to spend the afternoon in Mystic with him. I agreed. We stepped into a small restaurant on Main Street that had a tiny bay window with a table for two. We sat for hours, just talking. It had been years since I had met anyone who was so easy to be around. It was after that meeting that I remembered the script from my earlier meeting with the psychic: You will marry Ted. "Hmm," I thought. "What should I make of this?"

My birthday was coming up the following week and Tadashi asked me to come and stay at his home for the night. He lived in Monroe, on the other side of the state. I said yes and made my plans for my fiftieth birthday.

My children took me to the Lighthouse Inn in New London for dinner. It was luxurious. I told them, at dinner, that I was driving to Tadashi's home in Monroe after we left the restaurant. They weren't a bit keen on the idea. Glen was especially aghast. I told him that I was now fifty and was going to do what pleased me. Actually, I had done what pleased me for most of my life. I certainly wasn't going to change that on my fiftieth birthday.

Tadashi had given me directions that were incorrect and I got lost. Needless to say, I found my way, arriving about an hour later than expected. He greeted me with two lovely gifts and made my day end on a wonderful note. Well, it was more than that actually.

Tadashi had started to come to Preston to help me install new electrical lines in the basement. He was an electrical engineer and knew a bit about installing electricity. Ted number one was still working, and I decided that I better introduce them. It went well. Thank God!

Ted was wrapping up work on the two new front bathrooms. It wouldn't take long, and he would be returning to Minnesota. The fixtures were in and the tile work was just about complete. That is when he told me that there was no way he could get the Buick Roadmaster back home. He also told me that he was going to give the car to a person he had met at the restaurant down the street. I was furious but kept my feelings to myself. He still couldn't quite get it that he had a son who might like to have the car.

That week the man he was going to give the car to told him he didn't want it, so Ted gave it back to me and asked for $1,600 in place of the car for the work he had done. It was all the cash I had, but he had given me so much more. I was astounded that he had asked for so little. I withdrew all of my money from the bank and gave it to him. This was to be the first of several times that I sold my Buick Roadmaster.

Before Ted left for Minnesota, he went to see our daughter, Holly, nearby in Waterford, Connecticut. On his way back to Captain Grant's, he had his truck radio tuned to his favorite Norwich station. As he turned off Interstate 395 onto Route 2A, he saw a rather large delegation of people by the off ramp. The radio station was live at the goings-on. They announced that Congressman Gejdenson had just dedicated the Last Green Valley Corridor. They also talked about federal grants that were being given to small businesses that were historic and run by the owners who had done a restoration of the property. These grants were matching grants. The federal government would pay half and the recipient would pay the other half.

The front lawn of Captain Grant's was a mess. The original front stone wall was covered completely with dirt, and the dirt was covered with weeds. It was not a good presentation for a bed and breakfast. If we were successful, the grant would be used for restoration of the front of the property.

Ted said that Tadashi and I should try for the grant. We talked about it on the weekend, and on Monday morning Tadashi called me from work. He had spoken with Gejdenson's office. Yes, there was a matching grant. However, the grant application window was due to close that Thursday. "Oh God," I said. "Can we get this done?" Ted said that he would handle all of the paperwork. I would do everything else. I had to get two bids from contractors. I called Stonecroft, another bed and breakfast, and asked them if they would let their landscaper give us a bid. I then went to our local greenhouse and got a price on plants and grass seed.

Tadashi sent me the proposal, and on Thursday morning I was ready to go to the Last Green Valley office. It was thirty miles away and only 10:00 a.m., so I had plenty of time. My daughter was with me, and we thought we would make it an adventure. We could have lunch together and do a bit of antique shopping.

It was an adventure all right—we got lost! Neither of us ever got lost. The deadline for the proposal was 4:00 p.m. I was beginning to panic. It was after 3:00 and we still couldn't find the place. We stopped at a gas station and they had no idea where this place was. Street signs didn't help. We took a turn on an unlikely street and there it was. I entered the Last Green Valley building at 3:45 p.m. There were three women there. One of them said, "Sorry, but you are too late." Then they all laughed.

On Friday we got the call that we had won the grant. With the extra money from the grant we were able to sculpt the front yard, reseed the lawn, and plant almost a hundred feet of rose bushes. In the front of the original stone wall, the debris and weeds were removed and pea rock was added in their place. The once sad-looking front landscape was nearing beautiful.

In October 1996, Ted returned to Minnesota. Our relationship had changed. I had respect for him and all of the personal changes that he had made in his life. I wished him well.

The Buick Roadmaster remained on my front lawn and the sign was again put on the car. After a couple of days, a woman stopped by and wanted to buy the car on payments of $100 a week. It was to be a birthday surprise for her husband. We signed a contract and she gave me a $100 down payment. If she stopped making payments, the car would remain in my name. After eight payments I stopped getting money. About a month later I received a letter from San Diego. Her husband had been transferred from the New London submarine base in Connecticut and she wouldn't be getting the car. The $800 was mine to keep. I was no longer receiving unemployment and was existing on the small bit of rental income that I was taking in.

I had to sell the car, so I ran an ad in the local newspaper. I guess it was time to let the car go. I finally sold it to a man who I thought would give it tender loving care. He was disabled and would work on the car at his leisure. So now I had two more complete bedrooms, $800 from the car's first buyer, and another $2,400 from the final sale of the Buick. What a car! Thank you!

That winter Tadashi asked me if I needed him to make anything for the bed and breakfast. I thought about what I needed most, and two four-poster canopy beds came to mind. I was shocked at myself for mentioning something so grand, but I was even more stunned when he agreed to make them. For an electrical engineer, woodworking was just a hobby. He had to buy equipment and then there was the wood. It was cherry and came to an astounding $1,500 for just two queen-size beds. Throughout the winter we worked on the beds together in Tadashi's Monroe home. Our relationship was getting stronger as we were getting to know each other.

Spring was almost here. One Sunday I drove to Monroe to be with Tadashi. I had no guests and thought this would be a good time to get away from the business. I pulled into his driveway, got out of the car, and gasped. The house across the street on the left-hand side was being painted green. My mouth dropped open. The psychic had been right. It had been many months since I had visited the psychic and was told about Ted and the green house across the street. When I returned home, I pulled out my notes from that session to see what else she had told me. I was amazed. Tadashi was the one.

I had planned to open two more rooms in May. That meant going in front of the Preston zoning board once again. I was surprised to discover that they were not at all interested in having more than two bedrooms in a bed and breakfast. There were now two other bed and breakfasts in town, and they were also owned by women. I contacted the owners to see if they were interested in enlarging their available space. They both said yes. It would benefit all three of us if we could have access to more income from our businesses.

I decided that, given the reluctance of the board to let us have four rooms, we should go for eight instead. The meeting was a typical zoning board meeting. Nobody chuckled or laughed. They asked a lot of questions. One board member said, "We just don't need these cheap little hotels all over town." It was obvious that we were not getting any support.

Then one member put his thumbs in his suspenders, stood up, and said, "Let's not have the little women work so hard. Let's give them four rooms." It passed and now the three little women at the meeting could go to their homes and enlarge their businesses. The zoning regulations had just changed. We could now all have four rooms.

April arrived, and Easter Sunday was not far off. I got a call from a prospective guest and filled my current two bedrooms for the holy weekend. The next day, my son called and said that he had also filled the two rooms. I phoned Tadashi at work and told him that I had to set up the two new rooms right away. We were going to have four couples and we had only two rooms. We loaded the four-poster beds into my Acura hatchback and headed back across the state to Preston. The beds come totally apart and are just a pile of lumber until you set them up.

After trying the beds out in different rooms, I finally made my mind up and chose the Elizabeth and Amy rooms for the four posters. As I write this twenty years later, Tadashi still remembers the bed fiasco: assemble, disassemble, set up in another room, and so on.

Later that year, the weekend before Memorial weekend, I had only two rooms rented. At 8:30 in the morning, a half hour before breakfast, my guests came down to the kitchen. Their heads were wrapped in towels and they didn't look at all happy. "We have run out of water," one of them said. Sure enough, when I turned on the kitchen tap, nothing happened. I was out of water. I informed the guests that the well was probably slow and that I wouldn't use any water until the reserve tank was full. We decided to have breakfast, which would give the well about an hour to catch up. The guests would be able to finish showering after that.

Besides feeling downright humiliated, I was very concerned about the water situation. The following weekend I would have all four rooms full and not enough water to service my guests. Where was my help from the universe?

After breakfast Tadashi and I talked about what we would do. Option one: we could get a tanker to come in and backfill the well. Option two: we could get a tanker to come in and stay in the driveway while supplying water directly to our tank in the basement. Option three: we could tell the guests that they had nowhere to stay. We had to do something. Foxwoods Casino was open and the area was being overwhelmed with travelers every weekend. Memorial weekend would be even worse. There would be nowhere to send our guests.

The next morning Tadashi drove to the other side of the state and returned to his job. At 11:00 a.m. he called me and said, "What are you going to do?"

I said, "I'm going to pray to St. Anthony to help me find water." With my next breath, my jaw dropped open. I was standing in the kitchen doorway looking out the dining room window when a well rig came up my driveway. I said to Tadashi, "You won't believe what just came up the driveway: a well rig."

"What is it doing there?" he asked.

"I don't know, but I'm going to go find out. I'll call you back."

"Don't let it get away," he responded.

I went to the driver's side of the rig. The driver rolled down the window. He said hi and informed me that they were there to put in the well. I said, "How much is this going to cost?"

"Whatever is on your contract," he said.

"Could you please call the office and find out what the contract says?"

The driver answered, "Don't you want a well? We have the permit and moving this rig is very hard to do."

"Yes, I want a well. I just don't remember signing a contract with anyone."

I told them that I would wait for them inside the house until they finished their phone call. I paced back and forth in the dining room, looking out the window at the rig every minute or two. It took a grueling fifteen minutes for them to come into the house. I had the men sit at the dining room table and tell me what they found out.

"Well, there seems to be a problem. The office can't find a contract and they don't know how this mistake was made. Do you need a well?"

I answered in the affirmative but told them I had to work out a price with the office. The last thing they wanted to do was move the well rig. The last thing I wanted was for them to move the well rig.

For the next hour I negotiated a price with the main office for the new well. I decided to pay per foot for the digging instead of a set fee. I hoped they would find water not too far into the ground. Oh yes, I was still praying harder than ever. I couldn't believe what was happening. They had a drawing of my property from city hall and they had pulled a permit. Then the well bit broke. They got a new bit from wherever headquarters was and began digging again the following day.

My backyard was a muddy mess. There was no longer any grass from the well to the driveway, only mud. On Tuesday they reached bedrock, and by Wednesday I had a 24-gallon-a-minute well gushing out of the ground. I was ecstatic. They only had to go down 110 feet. Then they had the water tested by a lab. It was pure artesian well water.

It took me a long time to stop saying thank you to St. Anthony. All of my prayers were being answered. I made certain that I didn't ask for anything frivolous. Some will call this a coincidence, but I call it a downright miracle.

Chapter 5
NEW BEGINNINGS

That summer Tadashi and I continued to work on the bed and breakfast. Tadashi would come to Preston on Friday night and then leave for work at 5:30 on Monday morning, driving an hour and a half to reach Norwalk. If I had a day without guests, I would go to Monroe and spend the night with him. That was also an hour-and-a-half drive. We now talked every day, sometimes several times a day. I was beginning to worry about our relationship. I was becoming too dependent on him. If we broke up, I would be at such a loss of what to do. I decided I needed to talk to him.

It had been a year since we started dating, and Tadashi asked me out to a very fine restaurant to celebrate being together. We were by ourselves in a small nook. I decided to talk about our future together. I was so nervous, it was a wonder I didn't fall off my chair. I said that we should think about commitments. If he didn't want that, then we should both think of seeing other people. He didn't say a word. About fifteen agonizing minutes of small talk went by. Then he threw his arms into the air and said in a loud voice, "I'm ready."

I said, "Ready for what?"

He said, "To get married."

I was breathless.

The following day Tadashi called me from work with a suggestion. We had a trip planned to go to Las Vegas in September. He said, "Let's get married while we're there." He made all the arrangements. My job was to find a dress.

On September 12, 1996, we were married in a small chapel at the Flamingo Hotel. I will never forget the service. The minister asked for commitments between us that spoke to what marriage is truly meant to be. It was beautiful.

Throughout the year between us meeting and getting married, Tadashi and I would visit the casino about once a week. I always won. Tadashi loved to play cards and was very impressed with my ability to win. I knew that eventually I would stop winning. "Everyone stops winning," I would say to him.

Well, on the way back to our room at the Flamingo he said, "Let's stop at the blackjack table and see if you can still win."

The charm was gone. The winning stopped. We both wonder about that. He loves repeating the story to guests. How was it that I won for a year and then on our wedding day I lost? Actually I had just won the best husband in the world.

We returned home and took off our wedding bands. We were both afraid our families would be terribly hurt if we didn't have a wedding ceremony with everyone present. We announced to our families that we were going to be married in November. On November 30, we were married for the second time, at St. James Church, with two of our favorite priests attending. My daughter,

Holly, and Tadashi's son, Steve, were maid of honor and best man. We would not live together for another six years.

All went well the following year. Tadashi lived in Monroe due to his job being on the other side of the state and I lived in Preston running the bed and breakfast. We saw each other on the weekends, when Tadashi would arrive to help me with the business. If I had no guests, I would go to Monroe and stay with him.

We continued to work on the bed and breakfast. Tadashi tackled the electrical in the basement, which was hanging at neck height throughout the space. I continued to refinish furniture, paint, plaster, and accomplish whatever I could.

It was 1998, and when spring arrived we decided to go back to the zoning board and get a permit for four more rooms and a dinner restaurant. We anticipated a big fight and we got it. We were turned down with a flat NO. I was told that I could attend a meeting of the zoning board where they discussed the town and permits that people wanted.

I went to my first meeting and sat at the opposite end of the room. I was asked why I was there. I told them that they had invited me. To say that I was treated like a pariah was putting it mildly. I became so angry, I think I may have had steam coming out of my ears. I rose from my chair, walked over to their table, and slammed my fist down. I reminded them that the public zoning board meetings were taped. I then reminded them about the comment that had been made by one of their members previously regarding the "little women in town." I almost scared myself. The chairman said that they would work with me but I had only one more chance to go in front of the board.

Needless to say, my anxiety level was through the roof. Tadashi and I began to make plans for how we would precede with our decision to expand. We hired an attorney. Next we visited our local pastor for support. We decided to abandon the dinner restaurant. That would make our next attempt with the zoning board more palatable to them. We also decided to ask for sixteen rooms. We didn't really want that number but were pretty certain that if we asked for eight we would be stuck with four.

Finally the night arrived to face the zoning board once again. I was a bundle of nerves. We met our attorney at city hall. He informed us that he thought he could not help us. Father Cannon, our local priest, also came to the meeting to lend his support to us. We were the last on the docket. In fact, we were after Foxwoods Casino. The town had no love for the casino. I told Tadashi, "This is a bad omen."

It was nearing midnight when our request came up. Our attorney spoke, but it did no good. Then Father Cannon spoke in our favor and that didn't do any good. He had lived in town some twenty-odd years and still was not considered a local. Our neighbor from across the street also came to the meeting. His name was Mike and he had pneumonia and a high fever that day. He told us that we would never get the permit if he didn't stay. He spoke last. He told them that I had done more for Poquetanuck Village than anyone had done in many years and they were being stupid if they didn't give me the permit. With that statement Mike sat down. I think they were stunned. After a few seconds they talked among themselves and delivered their verdict: bed and breakfasts in Preston could have up to eight rooms.

Mike was one of them, an original Preston resident. The board members believed him, and I am eternally grateful for what he did that night.

We then completed our fifth bedroom and began to look at the home next door. That is where I lived. There were two rooms in the Avery house that I wished to make into additional bed and breakfast rooms. The Avery home was built in 1790 and was on the National Register of Historic Places. It was modestly built. The ceiling height was only six and a half feet. What it did have were two wood-burning fireplaces. They would be a draw for guests, BUT we would have to go before the zoning board again. This home is also haunted. It is where the ghost at the original back door was photographed.

We steeled ourselves for the night when we would go before the board. It was now 1999 and I had been in business for four years. This gave me some credibility, I thought. Just the same, we were worried.

We sat in front, on folding chairs, directly facing the zoning officials. Our request was heard rather quickly. I grabbed Tadashi's hand and whispered, "Here we go."

"So you want to have two bedrooms to rent in the home next to Captain Grant's," the official said.

"Yes," I said.

"The board would like to know if you will do as good a job on that house as you did on the Congdon house."

"Yes, of course," I responded.

"I think we are ready to vote." He looked at the other board members and they nodded in the affirmative. "All those in favor." Every hand but one went up.

Tadashi and I were stunned. I thought that perhaps we had finally earned their confidence in running a bed and breakfast.

Chapter 6
HAUNTED REALITY

It was in 1999 that it started to get difficult to hide the fact that Captain Grant's was haunted. There were many questions from guests about hearing people walk up the staircase, but there wasn't any sound when they hit the upstairs hallway and they didn't walk back down. There were also questions about children playing outside of the rooms in the middle of the night. They said there were balls rolling in the attic. Then there was the banging on the front door, which was quite frequent in the beginning days of the bed and breakfast. We offered no explanations. Most of the guests just passed it off as the behavior of other rude guests who were staying in the home at the same time.

A New York City detective transformed our silence into a slow acknowledgment of the home's spirits. He came downstairs before breakfast demanding his money back. When I asked him what had happened, he said that we were the two rudest innkeepers he ever met. I just knew in my heart of hearts that the spirits had done something. Indeed they had. Between 4:00 and 5:00 a.m. they had walked in the attic above the guest's room. The spirits were now exposed. We had to acknowledge their presence or start losing business.

We never advertised the spirits, but we no longer denied them. If a guest asked, "Is the house haunted?" we would say, "Do you want it to be or not?" We lost a few potential guests who were too afraid of spirits to take a chance on staying. Most of our guests were just plain curious about the goings-on. As long as I was able to continue to fill rooms with visitors, I was happy.

The year 2001 was becoming our best ever. Then on 9/11 that all came to a complete stop. All of our guests canceled. I was glued to the television. What was going to happen to our future and the nation's future? It was difficult to think with a clear head.

I got a call from a group in Paris who planned on coming for a stay in September. They were very gracious. The gentleman said, "We will come as soon as the planes are allowed to fly again." I also got a call from a party in New Hampshire who said they would never come. They were too afraid that the nuclear power plant in Connecticut would be targeted.

Everyone seemed to know someone who knew someone who had died on 9/11. When guests did visit, that was the main topic of conversation. There was much anguish and strong feelings of helplessness around the breakfast table.

In October we began to get steady reservations again, and by November our bed and breakfast was packed nearly every day. New Yorkers were fleeing the city to get a respite from the devastation. In fact, Connecticut businesses did very well that fall. I felt guilty and other people I talked to also felt guilty. We were experiencing a boom from the tragedy in our neighboring state. We did our best to make our guests feel at home. We listened and then listened some more, over and over. Our Paris guests arrived and shared stories about the reaction of the French to 9/11. As promised, the group from New Hampshire never did visit.

By January 2002 life was beginning to look somewhat more normal. The boom of the fall turned into the bust of the winter. By spring I was looking forward to summer and rooms full of guests. I wasn't thinking much about the spirits, and most of my praying was for help for others. I was in a personal slump along with my business and the country. I believe that Captain Grant's spirits knew the agony of our guests and focused on being supportive entities.

What I didn't know at that time was that the spirits were trying to help me be successful. An invisible group of twelve was hard at work. They liked having guests and they liked to be known.

The summer of 2002 gave me some unexpected publicity. The head of the Norwich Chamber of Commerce recommended Captain Grant's to HGTV. When HGTV phoned and asked me if I would be interested in having my home on the series *If Walls Could Talk*, I was stunned. We qualified because of three things: our bed and breakfast was historic, it had been renovated, and we were the people who had done the renovations. Trying to sound nonchalant I said, "I would be delighted." When I hung up the phone, I immediately called Tadashi. "We're going to be on national television. We're going to be on HGTV. Hallelujah! Thank you, God."

When the film crew showed up, there were just two of them, a camera operator and a reporter. They spent from 10:00 a.m. to 6:00 p.m. filming and asking me questions. I thought it was a long day. They thought it went remarkably fast.

Once the episode aired, I expected throngs of guests to show up at my door. Well, that didn't happen. What it did do was give me authenticity. Captain Grant's had been recognized as a truly historical home by the media. We still weren't focused on the hauntings.

I received an e-mail from the travel site BedandBreakfast.com in the fall. They were looking for specials that they would send to the *New York Times*. "What the heck," I thought. "I'll give it a try." I had three areas to choose from: Valentine's Day, Christmas, or Halloween. I decided on Halloween. I wrote a poem about our Halloween special and asked future guests to join us. I sent it off, and a half hour later I got a call from the site. They loved what I had written and had sent it off to the *Times*. Again, I was excited. More publicity. But the *Times* sat on the special and didn't publish it. "Oh well," I thought. "Easy come, easy go."

In 2003 the *Times* decided to put my special on their website. All of the calls I had expected a year earlier came pouring in. It was phenomenal. The *Times* had put us on the map. I was on a Montreal radio station as well as numerous other stations in our vicinity. The *Boston Globe* called. A newspaper from Long Island called. I was getting about three to four calls a day from various newspapers and radio stations. This lasted for about two weeks. It was all because Captain Grant's is haunted.

In October *USA Today* did a spread on haunted inns, and there was Captain Grant's, along with two other bed and breakfasts.

On Halloween, my husband and I were having dinner when the phone rang. It was 6:50 p.m. The woman on the other end of the line said, "Hello. I am calling from *CNN Headline News*. I want to inform you that we are featuring Captain Grant's on the news at 7:10 p.m."

I hung up the phone and called as many relatives as I could. Then my husband and I sat glued to the television. The woman who called had said there would be three haunted bed and breakfasts talked about. The first bed and breakfast was mentioned and pictured, with about fifteen seconds being given to the spot.

Then it was Captain Grant's turn. We expected a presentation similar to the first one. That didn't happen. The reporter started talking and just kept on talking. "There are ghosts running all over the place in this house. You go around a corner and you could run right into one." My husband and I started laughing. We didn't know if this would scare future guests away or not, but it was downright hilarious. The third bed and breakfast never got aired. There wasn't enough time after Captain Grant's was on.

Then we began getting calls from ghost hunters wanting to do paranormal investigations. At first I was in awe of them. That wore off quickly. A typical phone call went somewhat like this: "I am Joe from Dark Ghost Investigators. We would like to do an investigation of your place. We need two rooms and access to the Adelaide room and we will not charge you for that service."

It was hard not to laugh. My typical response was something like this: "Joe, we would love to have you come and investigate. However, you need to pay for your rooms, and if someone is in Adelaide you can't go in there. [Adelaide is our most haunted room.] You also can't turn off all the lights if we have other guests."

Then I would usually hear something like this: "Uh, we don't have a lot of money, but I'll talk to my group and get back to you."

Most groups who call are young people in their late teens and early twenties and don't have the funds to spend. Still, many groups did come and continue to come to this day. Most of them don't have a theory about the phenomena they are witnessing. Some have firm beliefs about what they are witnessing. It is an ongoing process for all of them, as it is for us as well. Some of the groups have psychics, some have sensitives, and some are just curious.

We started getting on ghost Internet sites, Facebook, etc. One group came to stay and put up about an hour-long video of Captain

Grant's and our ancient cemetery behind the home on one of the social media sites. We found out about it a few months later.

In 2010 we got a call from the producer of *Psychic Kids: Children of the Paranormal*, a series that aired on the A&E network. Again, we had been chosen for a nationally aired television show. This was quite different from HGTV. I remember that there were about eleven members of the cast and crew. It was very impressive. We were to be episode eight of season two. There were three psychic children and three parents, the producer, the director, and the rest of the A&E crew. Kim Russo was the adult psychic who helped the children. She was awesome and was hired to take the place of Chip Coffey, the original host.

When Kim arrived by limousine, I was told by the producer that nothing had been revealed to her about where she was headed. I met her at the front door and we shook hands. She then said, "I sense a Mercy here and she's not happy about her name." I was flabbergasted. Nobody had that information. It wasn't on our website or in any of our advertising. We have a room called Adelaide. Adelaide is Mercy Adelaide Grant. I didn't name the room Mercy because I didn't think it was appropriate.

Kim and I went up the stairs, and one by one she gave me all the names for the rooms. I am still in awe of her.

The psychic children from the show had all experienced different degrees of difficulties in their lives because of their paranormal abilities. The eldest female child was having a difficult time controlling a spirit that followed her wherever she went. While exploring the attic at Captain Grant's, she had the opportunity to tell the spirit in the attic to go away. It was her first experience at taking control.

All three children were afraid of the "man in the attic." The youngest female child told me the following morning after their visit, "We told him to go away, and there he went, right through the wall." The children also told me that this ghost had been mean to children when he was alive. I had been told this about that spirit from someone else who had visited earlier. She was a sensitive.

The only male child from the show was a medical intuitive. While at Captain Grant's, he told me that I had knee pain. I said no, but that wasn't true. What I did tell him was that I had pain in my back. He did Reiki on the area where I ached and the pain disappeared for nine months. This exhausted him, as I found out myself later when I experienced exhaustion after a communication session with Adelaide.

To this day I wish that I had some contact with those psychic children. I think of them often. By now they are young adults.

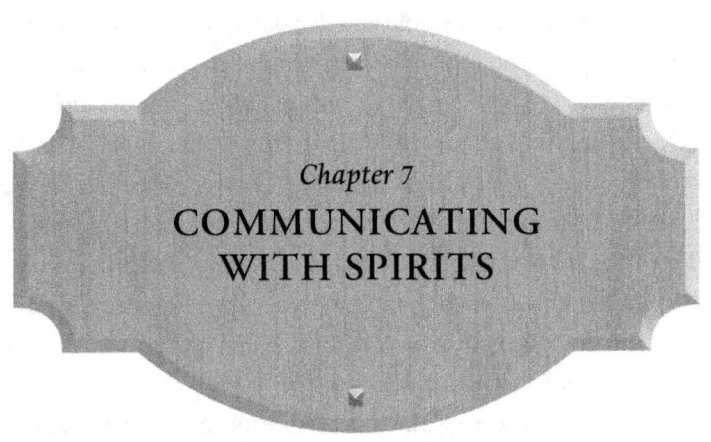

Chapter 7
COMMUNICATING WITH SPIRITS

Shortly after *Psychic Kids* aired, we had a family stay with us who were ghost hunters. They were not the typical ghost hunter types that usually stayed with us. There was a mother and a father and their child. They followed around a paranormal research group called Scientific Paranormal. I had been told that Scientific Paranormal was an offshoot group of the TV series *Ghost Hunters* and had conducted an investigation into the paranormal at Captain Grant's the week before. The members of Scientific Paranormal were scientists by day and ghost hunters by night. One of the parents explained that they tried to go wherever Scientific Paranormal went because of the excellent reputation that this particular group has. The couple figured that if that group went somewhere and they followed, maybe they would also find spirits. Other than being ghost hunters, the family were just our usual visitors. The unusual happened at breakfast the following morning.

The guests had finished eating and were chatting about life in general, probably politics or the state of affairs with the government.

These are two of the more popular subjects guests like to chat about. One couple rose from the table and decided to return to their room. My husband and I took the opportunity to sit down at the table with our other guests. This changed the entire flow of conversation.

Guests began to ask us about the spirits in the house. Who was here? Why were they here? What did they want? I had no answers for them. All I knew was that the home had mysterious happenings and we decided it was in the form of spirits since so many mysterious incidents had occurred. This was followed by my husband and I trying to figure out what caused these occurrences. All of our research had been to no avail.

We attempted to explain to our guests the Adelaide shower curtain debacle (we had replaced over six curtain rods in that room due to their flying off the wall), knocking at the front door (it was more like pounding), and boots stomping in the attic, and then waited for our guests to respond. We smiled, felt foolish, and thought, "They must think we are just plain nuts."

The ghost hunter family had quite a lot to say. The mother—I'll call her Rose—said that she could communicate with the spirits but her husband and daughter could not. Everyone became quite interested in what she had to say. I asked her how she was able to accomplish this. Most of us thought that she must hear them in her head or some other way that we couldn't understand. This was not the case. She used L-rods, or divining rods, to speak with the spirits. I asked her if she had brought them to Captain Grant's, and indeed she had. I requested that she get them from her room and demonstrate them for us. She agreed and soon we were all anxiously awaiting we knew not what.

There were eight of us at the table. We all sat silently waiting for what would happen next. Rose held the rods straight out, one in each hand, with her elbows on the table, and sat very still. She recited a short prayer and then introduced herself to the spirits. Calmly, she asked if anyone from the spirit world would talk to her. She told the spirits that if an answer was no, the rods would cross, and if the answer was yes, the rods would open wide. She stated her name. "I am Rose. Will you talk to me?" The rods opened wide. I watched her hands closely. They did not appear to move. Then Rose asked, "Are you a female?" The rods stayed open. To be certain of the answer, she then said, "Are you a male?" and the rods crossed. And so the questions went for about a half hour.

One of the other guests asked if she could use the rods. Eventually all of the guests wanted to see if the rods would work for them. One by one each guest had their turn. First a man named John tried, then his wife, Sylvia. The rods pointed straight ahead. Then my husband, Tadashi, was convinced by the guests to give it a try. Again the rods pointed straight ahead and did not move. They responded to no one but Rose. Because I have had so many unusual occurrences in my life, I thought maybe they would work for me.

Rose handed me the rods, and before I could do anything they began to spin like helicopter blades. I dropped them on the table, breathed heavily, secured my elbows, and picked up the rods. I forgot to pray. The rods were spinning fast. I was afraid that I would be hit in the face. The rods were quite long and I have short arms. Then they began to slow down. I told the spirits my name. I asked the same questions that Rose had. I was astonished and shaken. They responded to me as if I had done this all my life. "Oh my God," I sighed. Now what?

I thought about buying a set of L-rods after that but could not get myself to send in an order for them. My religious beliefs were against conjuring. I have read the Bible, and Christ told his followers not to conjure up evil. Was this conjuring and were the spirits evil?

I felt certain that the spirits were benign, but I was so confused. I thought, "The spirits are here. Should I talk to them? Do I really have a gift, or is this just my ego speaking? Why me? I'm just an ordinary person."

I was in a spiritual fight with myself and I did nothing about getting divining rods. Five weeks passed and I had given up on ordering the rods. Then on a Monday a package from Rose arrived. I knew it was the rods. I just stood there staring at the package. What should I do? Open the package? Throw them away? Put them away unopened? Feeling really stupid about my quandary, I decided to open the package. When I finally got through the wrapping, there was a long felt bag. I nervously opened the bag and held the rods. They hummed. Again, I dropped the rods. Now what?

"Go on," I said to myself. They were copper, with a brass sleeve over the short end of the *L*. I was in awe that a guest would send them to me and decided to honor her generosity by trying them out. They worked as well as they had the first time. After a few minutes I put them back in the gray bag.

Almost a year passed without my using the rods more than a half dozen times. I had to resolve my inner battle concerning my religious beliefs. I finally accomplished this with help from a Catholic priest who was a guest at the inn. He said to me, "St. Paul and St. Peter are spirits. Are they evil?" That was all it took to resolve my dilemma.

In 2011 I decided to offer our guests a Groupon with a ghost communication session added for free. (Midweek days in the winter months are hard to fill.) The Groupon company stated that it would never sell. They wanted me to give a free bottle of wine with each reservation. I told them, "I already give complimentary wine, beer, and soda. That's no more incentive than what I already do." Finally Groupon relented and agreed to the ghost communication lesson. One hundred and thirty-five rooms sold out in thirty-six hours, and that was the beginning of many spirit sessions, as well as the start of many calls from Groupon asking me to do more specials.

I have done three of these Groupon specials but don't plan to do any from now on. I do continue to give the spirit communication lessons if guests put in a request.

The ghost communication lesson includes use of the L-rods. The guest or guests and I meet in either our dining room or the game room, whichever has more privacy at the time. I have two sets of rods that I use, one for myself and one for the guests. We sit in a circle around a table. I usually start by asking guests to share what they have already experienced with the paranormal. I then show them the rods and ask each of them to hold them. This is so that the participants know the rods would be difficult to control. Then I begin to ask questions, mostly about the people who are present. Each guest is given a chance to try to communicate using the rods. It is great fun, but guests have also cried and been stunned, and non-believers often begin to doubt their belief that there is no afterlife.

During these communication sessions, some guests have been told that their deceased loved ones are happy and don't want to return to the land of the living. Almost every guest has asked about their own fate. Unfortunately the spirits have told me that they do not know the future. They only know the past. (I address this issue later on in the section on time in chapter 22.) This means our destiny is up to us. I believe that if we are doing what we are meant to do on this earth, the path of our future will proceed smoothly, with few bumps and bruises. If we choose the wrong path, it may be filled with briars and lessons that we don't want to learn through experience.

I have learned extensively about the spirit life. Now I wish to share what I have learned with all of you, my readers.

The following chapters are synopses of my interviews with the spirits that became such a large part of Captain Grant's. The full interviews are in the appendix.

Chapter 8
DEBORAH ADAMS

Deborah Adams was discovered by a family who rented Captain Grant's for a weeklong vacation. I gave them a ghost communication lesson and let them use my rods during the time they stayed at the inn. Only the women used the rods. The men were not interested. Of the five women, the rods responded to four of them. The fifth one declined to try for religious reasons. Every day I saw them out on the deck using the rods. (At that time I had only one pair of rods. Now I have rods for my guests to use and I keep mine for myself.)

On Thursday of that week the women invited me to sit outside and chat with them. They told me all about Deborah Adams. She was five years old when she died and was buried in the old cemetery behind the house. The old cemetery dates back to the mid-1600s. It was the first town cemetery. Currently no one owns it, not even the town. The only care it has received since 1954 is from the Boy Scouts one summer, members of the town cemetery commission, and a woman who comes once in a while on her own to try to clean it out. My husband and I have put a bit of money into the grounds, but it is a losing situation. Graves have sunk into the ground. It is overgrown with underbrush and vines. And now one end of the cemetery is collapsing. It is situated on high ground above a stream but is slowly giving way to nature. This is where Deborah Adams was interred.

I asked the family how they knew her name. One of the women, Barbara, said that they went through the alphabet. "Does your first name start with an *A*?" and so on until they got her name. What this family wanted to know was if they could try to find Deborah's grave. I decided to give it a try. I was still somewhat skeptical but thought, what the heck. "Let's go," I said.

I rounded up John, our groundskeeper, and asked him to get our large gas-powered weed trimmer and meet us in the field behind the house. The women and I met up with him halfway to the cemetery entrance. Barbara led the procession, with the rods pointing the way. We walked through ankle-high grass and not a word was spoken. It felt as if a sacred mission was being conducted in the middle of a bright, sunny summer afternoon.

After several minutes of walking, we could see the cemetery entrance. It lay between two stone walls that surrounded the plot of land. We stood about three feet in front of the wall opening and looked ahead. The cemetery was nearly impassable. Vines and bushes were everywhere. Bittersweet hung from the tops of fifty-foot trees. Different grasses and weeds were waist-high, and dead branches were scattered throughout. Between reeds of grass we could see headstones. Only two tall headstones stood out in the resting place of the last three hundred years. Both were family obelisks. All was silent but for a gentle breeze. It was truly a solemn gathering of souls.

John went through the entrance first. He cut some of the tall weeds on the ground and then held the larger vines back with his hand while we ducked our heads down to waist level and forged our way through. Once inside we saw that the cemetery was covered with weeds and bramble even worse than what we had first seen. If we weren't careful, thorns would stick into our arms or our clothing. I had told everyone to wear long pants, so we were somewhat prepared. I hadn't been out to the cemetery for months and was aghast at the condition it was in.

I checked with officials of the town later that week and discovered that they hadn't tended to the cemetery since 1954. Large trees grew everywhere. Bittersweet and grape vines climbed the trees, and the area was almost entirely shaded by foliage. We had to be careful not to trip over headstones. Some of them had sunk into the ground so far that we could no longer tell who the person was beneath the stone. All was silent but for the sound of footsteps.

Barbara walked closely behind John. He followed her every instruction and she was following the lead of the rods. "Turn slightly to the left," Barbara said. We continued to walk in a single file. "Now go ahead. Wait. Stop here." About twenty-five feet in, we came across a headstone that had "D. A." on it. Barbara asked Deborah if that was her stone. The rods made a severe cross for no and we moved on.

Not far ahead, as we angled to the left, the rods started spinning. I asked John to whack in a circle around the area. And there it was: a granite stone sunk in the ground so deep that only about eight inches of it was showing. We couldn't see a name. Barbara asked Deborah, "Is this your grave?" The rods indicated a resounding yes, pointing as far apart as they could. All seven of us stood there looking at the place where her bones lay buried. Prayers were said and then we silently left the cemetery, leaving behind a cleared path to Deborah's last resting place. I have been out there since that day and can no longer find the grave. It may have sunk below the ground.

Deborah is now the spirit I communicate with the most. She lived in the 1700s, was born in the month of October, and died of an illness when she was five years old. She told me that she never lived in the home, so I'm not certain why she is here now.

Deborah loves to play pranks and have other children around. Perhaps the most dramatic thing that she has done was interfere with a phone call that I had taken. A woman called to make a reservation. I took all the usual information from her and thought that this was a normal booking. Not so. On the date requested, the woman arrived with a child's tea set. I said to her, "That is very nice of you, but why did you bring this to me?"

She answered, "It was the little girl on the phone with us—Deborah. She asked me to bring her a tea set. I'm sorry that it isn't new. I just stopped at an antique shop along the road and picked it up."

I gasped. I told her that Deborah had died in the 1700s but that her spirit stays at Captain Grant's. The guest didn't know what to say.

"Didn't you hear her talking?" she asked. "It was very clear."

"No," I said. "The only voice I heard on the phone was yours." I couldn't believe it. The woman looked really shaken up. I know that I was!

The little tea set remains at Captain Grant's in the dining room, available for Deborah to play with whenever she wants. At times it is no longer where I put it but is found in another place in the house.

Deborah also likes to stir up trouble in the Adelaide bathroom. Her first trick was to have the shower curtain rod fly off the wall and hit a maid. Now this maid did have a rather nasty sense of humor, if you could call it humor at all. One morning she came downstairs and told me that the rod had flown off the shower wall and hit her in the head and she couldn't get the rod back in place. She was a smart woman, so I was a bit irritated to have to show her how to hang the rod back up. She insisted that I see the rod, so up the stairs I went and there was the rod now lying in the bedroom, not the bathroom. It was an old rod from the 1950s and was metal, with threaded adjusters at the ends. Each adjuster would move about an inch. I told her to watch me while I hung the rod. "Damn," I said. The rod was about a foot too short. The maid smiled at me with that "I told you so" expression.

I called my type-A engineering husband up to the Adelaide room and showed him what had happened. He searched everywhere for a missing piece of rod, even though the rod was not broken. It still had its ends on it. He said, "There has to be a part missing. This rod didn't just shrink. It is physically impossible." In the bedroom there is a round hole that a steam pipe once ran through. This hole goes to the first floor and then down to the basement. Well, Tadashi searched all three floors, under furniture and in areas away from the pipe hole. He finally gave up and went to the store and bought a new shower curtain rod.

That rod didn't last a week and came flying off the wall right in front of me. Then we bought another rod, with the same result. That is when my husband said, "I'm going to glue that thing in place so that it will never come off again." Ha! Within another month the new shower curtain rod was also found in the bedroom. We've gone through about six rods since that time. Deborah really does not like to have a shower curtain in the tub area.

Eventually Tadashi put a round piece of wood under the rod and screwed it to the wall, so now the current rod is glued and screwed to the wall. The old rod was used for years in our fire pit to stir ashes. The other rods were broken and thrown away.

Deborah has materialized to the naked eye only once in the years that Captain Grant's has been open. We once had a young girl named Amie working for us. Amie was an atheist. She believed that we're here and then we're not, so we should have fun while we can. She thought that all of the talk about ghosts was nonsense.

Well, Amie had been cleaning the Adelaide room every day for about a week. Then for three days in a row she found the metal mini blinds separated near the bottom of the window. It was as if someone small or on their knees had been looking out of the window. For two days Amie straightened out the blinds. On the third day Amie once again had her arms outstretched to fix the blinds when a little girl walked right through her arms. We could hear Amie's screams throughout the house. She came running downstairs, crying and screaming, "I'm going to die! I'm going to die!"

We attempted to calm her down to no avail. Finally we got her to tell us what had happened through ongoing bursts of sobs. She told us how the little girl had walked right through her arms and then disappeared into the bedroom. "She vanished," Amie said.

We sent her home. She refused to come back to work for three days and said that she would never go into that bedroom again. She did, of course, after a respectable amount of time, and sometime later she became a born-again Christian. So much for living, dying, and then it's all over!

Deborah has also been caught on camera and several times on an EVP (electronic voice player). She has been heard repeatedly by the human ear. Guests often hear her giggling in the hallway or rolling balls in the attic. No one has gotten words or a sentence from her.

One female guest awoke around 2:00 a.m. one night and had the urge to take a picture. She shot the photo in the direction of the bathroom, and lo and behold there was Deborah peeking around the corner of the doorway. She was quite small and looked to be more like a three-year-old child than a five-year-old.

I could go on for hundreds of pages about Deborah, but that would not be fair to the other spirits that occupy Captain Grant's. So I have one last story about Deborah to share with you before moving on.

We had a couple reserve the Adelaide room. The man who made the booking knew the room was haunted, but his partner did not. The partner said later that he would not have come if he had known about the spirits. The morning after they arrived, one of the men came downstairs and gave me one of the biggest hugs I have ever had. He was so excited, jabbering and arms flailing around. "What happened?" I asked. He sat down at the dining room table, the other guests listening with rapt attention.

In the middle of the night, the two men were woken by a sound from the bathroom similar to a fork lightly hitting leaded glass. *Ting, ting.* The one man crawled under the covers and stayed there, scared as all get out. His partner, full of curiosity, got out of bed and headed for the bathroom. He turned on the light and looked at the shower curtain. One by one, the rings had come off the shower curtain rod and were being placed across the remaining part of the rod. This was making the shower curtain face backward.

That man was one of the happiest guests we have ever had. By the way, both gentlemen have returned to stay with us. Their story is in a memory book that I keep in each room for guests to write in.

In order to learn more about the spirit world, I conducted interviews with seven spirits at Captain Grant's. The following summary is paraphrased from those interviews. The full interviews are found in the appendix of this book.

Synopsis of My Interview with Deborah

I begin each interview by saying who I am, even though the spirits know who I am at this point. When I contact Deborah, the rods fly around in circles and she gives me a "hug" (that is when one rod touches one of my cheeks and the other rod touches the other cheek). I ask Deborah, as well as all the other spirits that I interview, if it would be okay with them to be written about in this book. All agree.

I ask Deborah about the age of her spirit, and she tells me that the spirit continues to age even though it is eternal. One thing that surprises me is her no answer to the question "Have you ever met anyone in the spirit world that you knew when you were alive?" It is quite common for spirits to be reincarnated surrounded by spirits that they knew in a past lifetime. (To give you an example of this, I recently used the rods to answer some questions from one of my guests. She wanted to know about her husband in her last life. The spirits told me that her husband in that lifetime was English and that the two of them had moved to India. They also said that he was in the military. Well, her current husband is English and is in the military, and they were planning to move to India within a month.)

As it turns out, Deborah saw her parents go to a bright light and has not seen them since. Deborah also says that she is trapped in the house. This does not make sense to the Catholic side of me. According to the Bible, children are supposed to be innocents. She should ascend to heaven and not be reincarnated. I personally believe that Deborah is happy in the house and doesn't want to go anywhere.

Guests often hear children playing, so I ask Deborah if there is anyone in the house that she plays with. Her playmate turns out to be a young boy who died sometime in the early twentieth century.

Even though Deborah's spirit acts like a child, she possesses knowledge beyond her years. I wonder aloud if the spirits continue to learn from our world, and she answers in the affirmative. She remains in the house even though I have asked her to go to the light.

The little boy that Deborah plays with has been reported by several guests to be named John. I have never spoken to him. Supposedly he is in the cemetery across the street. This would make sense since he died in the early twentieth century and the old cemetery was no longer used at that time.

Chapter 9
DANIEL

The property that Captain Grant's sits upon was originally the John Pickett Farm. In 1707 John Pickett sold the land to a man named Samuel. In 1754 a descendant of Samuel's, either Zachariah or Samuel Jr., built the home now called Captain Grant's.

Daniel was a son of one of these men. I didn't know which one, so I decided to ask Daniel about it in an interview.

We first became aware of Daniel when guests reported hearing someone walking in the attic with heavy boots on. It usually happened around 4:00 a.m. I didn't know who it was or how to communicate with the spirit at that time. The incident that made us go public about our spirits involved Daniel.

As I recounted earlier, in 1998 a New York City detective reserved the Adelaide room for a Friday and a Saturday night. On Sunday morning he came down to the kitchen at 7:30 and asked for his rental money back. He clearly was not a happy man.

"What's wrong?" I asked.

"I think that you and your husband are two of the rudest innkeepers I have ever met."

"What did we do?"

"You know darn well what you did," he said vehemently.

I stood there with my mouth open, just looking at him and feeling numb. I think my lack of a response prompted him to tell me what had happened. He said that at 4:00 a.m. my husband had started walking back and forth in the attic above their bed with boots on. Apparently this had lasted for nearly an hour. He went on about his anger at being kept awake for the rest of the night.

I apologized. I knew this was it. The time had come to let the cat out of the bag. "Why did he have to be a detective?" I thought. Anyway, I considered alternative answers for a couple of seconds but decided that it was time to fess up. I said, "We have a ghost in the attic and I will prove it to you after breakfast," and then I held my breath again. I was certain that he would think I was nuts.

He didn't and told me that he would accompany me up to the attic after breakfast when the other guests had cleared off the breakfast deck.

An hour and a half later, breakfast was winding down. Guests were now mingling in the parlor. People were in the yard taking pictures, and the time had come to take the gentleman up to our attic.

We went up through the outside staircase and entered the attic through a side door. Turning to my left and looking toward the back of the home, I pointed down and said, "Your bedroom is right down there." He nodded and just stared at the floor. It was completely covered from end to end with eighteenth-century lumber stacked about two feet high. The lumber had been thrown on the floor in a haphazard way. It was obvious that no one could have been walking around on the floor. They wouldn't have been able to balance.

Our detective guest went downstairs and rebooked for our Halloween special. He stayed with us two times after that. Daniel continues to pace the attic floor, but now only on rare occasions.

The next big incident with Daniel happened when *Psychic Kids* filmed their show at Captain Grant's. The children's mentors took them up to the attic at night. Only flashlights were used. The children were scared. They said that a man who was mean to children when he was alive was occupying the attic. The adults instructed the children on how to get rid of a spirit such as the one they were encountering. They were counseled on how to take charge and were told that the spirit couldn't be in charge if they, the children, let the spirit know that he was not in charge. In this case the children ultimately took charge and sent Daniel away. Soon after, the children were led downstairs by their mentors. Daniel didn't return for nine months.

When I first started using the L-rods, I decided to talk to Daniel. Due to the historic survey that put Captain Grant's on the National Register, I knew the last names of the families that had lived in the house. This made it easy to get Daniel's last name. I asked if he was a Grant, and that was a no. Then I asked if he was a son of Samuel, and that is when I got a yes. I asked him a few more questions and decided to ask him if he had been mean to children when he was alive. The rods pointed straight ahead, and that was the end of Daniel talking to me. He was certainly unhappy and perhaps more than a little peeved. I apologized and went downstairs. That was the end of that interview. I didn't know if he would ever talk to me again.

I knew that Daniel was Samuel's descendant, but I had no idea what his first name was. One morning after breakfast, I was giving a ghost communication lesson when I got the name "Daniel." Previously, a guest at Captain Grant's had been out to the old cemetery and had found a grave marked with the name Daniel. So I figured it was the perfect time to find out if that was the spirit's first name.

When I asked the spirit if he would speak to me, he said yes. I asked him if his name was Daniel, and indeed it was. I also asked Daniel if he was trapped at Captain Grant's and he stated that he was. Actually he stated that he was trapped on the property that was owned by Samuel's family. That was a substantially larger piece of land than Captain Grant's is on today. Captain Grant's is currently about five acres in size. The original property was one hundred acres. This allowed Daniel to wander next door and to other nearby areas of Poquetanuck Village.

Daniel is now a constant spirit at the home and is more than willing to communicate with me. I believe that someday soon he will be reincarnated and then he will no longer be with us.

Before describing my interview with Daniel, I want to mention some things about spirits. They are not gods, saints, or fortune-tellers. You cannot see their expressions or hear their voices. The spirits at Captain Grant's consist of energy and claim to be souls. This makes it very difficult to know if they are telling the truth. In the case of Daniel, when I interviewed him, I was not sure if he was elaborating, telling the truth, or downright lying.

Synopsis of My Interview with Daniel

I had been researching the early owners of Captain Grant's and found that the original owner of the home was Samuel. Samuel had purchased the land in 1707.

For this interview, I sit in the kitchen and ask the spirits if Daniel could speak to me. The rods answer with a wide-apart yes.

The interview begins with a conversation about Daniel's family. He verifies for me that he was Samuel's son. I had long thought the original owners of the land were farmers due to having a hundred acres of land, but Daniel states that his father was a blacksmith and that the blacksmith shop was in the home next door. This is the current Avery house. I had been told that the front of the Avery house was originally from the 1600s. This was somewhat verified by knowing that two fires occurred in what is now the Holly room. The beams in this room are like iron after having being burned.

I wish to know about Daniel himself and guide the conversation in that direction. I suspect that the spirit of Daniel is a young man. This leads to questions about his age, how he died, and if he was ever married. It turns out that Daniel was twenty-one when he perished in an accident at his father's blacksmith shop. In his short life he managed to have two children with a woman who was married to another man. His parents never found out about the affair, and neither did the woman's husband.

Daniel believes that he will be reincarnated. It is now well over two hundred years since he was killed in the accident. I think that this might give him some credibility in the spirit world.

We talk about reincarnation, and Daniel states that it occurs if you have something to atone for or correct. He also states that the soul enters a child at the exact time of birth and leaves at the exact time of death.

The spirits need energy to communicate with us, and not everyone gives off enough energy for this to happen. Daniel verifies this theory as well as my question about electric shocks. I had a college professor tell me that most people who have contact with the spirit world have had a shock at some point in time. This is not a constant, since some psychics have an innate ability given to them at birth.

At this point I end the interview to make my husband dinner. I am given a hug by Daniel.

When we meet again, I ask Daniel more extensive questions about his affair. These questions and answers are in the appendix.

Since writing this chapter, we have had living descendants of Samuel stay with us. When I asked them if he was a farmer, they said no. I then asked them if he was a blacksmith. To my astonishment, they answered in the affirmative. Daniel had been telling me the truth.

Chapter 10
MERCY ADELAIDE GRANT

I have known about Mercy since I purchased the home she once resided in. She was Captain Grant's wife. Together they had three children, two boys and a girl.

I decided to name the guest bedrooms after women and chose Mercy to be the first room that I opened with. Now, this is not quite the way it went. I tossed around the idea of naming rooms after virtues but decided it just wasn't sellable enough. Prudence, Mercy, and Faith, plus other virtues, might actually turn some guests off. So I went with Adelaide, Mercy's middle name. It wasn't until several years later that I learned that she liked the name Mercy and not the name Adelaide for the bedroom named after her. Kim, the psychic who accompanied the children from *Psychic Kids*, actually told me that Mercy did not like the name Adelaide. I later found this to be true once I started using the L-rods.

Mercy is a powerful spirit. If she needs more energy to talk with you, she can take it at her will. Once I was giving guests a ghost communication lesson in the east parlor. There were about ten of us in the room. I was standing in front of a love seat and speaking to Mercy. Guests were all around me. Then I collapsed onto the loveseat with no warning. I was totally exhausted. I don't know if the other spirits at Captain Grant's can do this. She is the only one who has actually done it.

Mercy doesn't play tricks on anyone. She likes the male guests and is one of only two spirits in the home that will talk to men. If a guest looks like her husband, she may become quite enamored with him. She especially likes bearded men. If I am giving a ghost communication lesson and there is a man at the table with a beard and the spirit I am talking to is Mercy, she will want the rods to stay focused on that person. If I ask her to point the rods toward someone she likes, it is always a man with a beard if one is present. The men usually blush but not their wives.

Mercy has materialized in front of guests more than any spirit that is at the home. One guest actually drew a picture of her. We also had a maid who saw Mercy on the grand staircase and drew us a picture of her as well. Both drawings are very similar. (There are no pictures of any of the Grant family.) Mercy has been seen in the Adelaide room on several occasions, sometimes holding a child's hand in each of her hands. All of the sightings of Mercy have her in a blue dress.

During my conversations with Mercy, I became confused about something that she had said several times. When I asked her if she saw the light, she said she did but chose to stay in the house. I then asked her if she was waiting for Captain Grant. To this she answered yes. Now for the confusing part. I have talked to Captain Grant during a couple of conversations. So if Mercy is waiting for him, he's here. Why is she still waiting?

Then I learned, just this year, that the Captain Grant at Captain Grant's is her son and not her husband. Her husband died at sea when he was thirty-two years old. It was in a violent storm off Cape Hatteras, probably a hurricane. Their gravestones are in the new cemetery across the street. So I asked Mercy what I thought was a logical question: "Is your husband buried across the street in the town cemetery?" She said no. He was buried at sea, befitting a sea captain. It is sad to think of how lonely she must have been. I asked her to go to the light several times, but she wouldn't. Eventually she became annoyed with me for asking, so I stopped. Then I found out why.

Synopsis of My Interview with Mercy Adelaide Grant

"Mercy, I am writing a book and I want to have a chapter dedicated to you. Is this okay with you?"

"Yes."

"I have a quick question for you and then I have to tend to the B&B business. Can you come to my office next door for the interview?"

This interview in my office became somewhat bizarre. While interviewing Adelaide, she told me her husband had already been reincarnated—in the form of my husband Tadashi! None of this made sense to me, and I began to think that I was not interviewing Mercy but a spirit that was pretending to be Mercy. The reason for my suspicion was that I had been told earlier by a spirit that when we die, our spirit remains who we were in life until we are reincarnated into a new person. If this is the case, Mercy's husband is gone, and when my husband dies, his spirit will be him, Tadashi, and not Captain Grant.

I reread the interview many times and knew something was wrong but did not have the time to interview Mercy again. Then a twist of fate occurred. Living descendants of Captain Grant visited the bed and breakfast. I asked them some of the same questions that I had asked Mercy in our interview, but got different answers. They stated that Captain Grant never lived in Colchester. I was concerned about this because other relatives of Captain Grant had stayed with me in 1995 and what they told me jibed with what Mercy had said. Memory can easily be faulty and I set out to see if I could get more history of the Grants, but to no avail. I did find out that members of the Grant family lived in the home until the 1860s.

It was sometime later that I took the time to interview Mercy at the bed and breakfast. This was a very different interview. It cleared up many of the questions that I had about the first interview. It had not been Mercy that I had interviewed in my office that first time, but another entity. I don't trust the spirits in the home where I live and have since stopped communicating with them.

As it turns out, it was Mercy's family who lived in Colchester, although I don't know when that was.

In this second interview with the real Mercy, I got a bit carried away with my curiosity about the afterlife. I asked many questions that include God as the subject. I study Bible prophesy and wanted to ask her questions about what I have read about the end times. I also wanted to know about heaven and hell. It turns out that there is no hell as we have gotten to know it. There is no burning up in a sea of fire, but instead a dark, cold, isolated place with no love, no God, and no human contact. Reincarnation is a chance to redeem our misdeeds or lack of accomplishment and not end up there for eternity.

I asked questions about several subjects. One of them had to do with manifestation. I asked Mercy about spirits appearing during the day. As it turns out, they appear during the day as well as at night. We can see them more easily at night. So it is we who make the difference between seeing them at night or seeing them during the day. As energy, they don't have enough of a profile with their background and we see right through them, not seeing them at all.

I could have conversed with Mercy for hours. I believe that I can trust what she tells me. She has yet to falter, to tell me something that makes no sense or tell me something and then reverse her story later on. It is one of the cues that I look for in my interviews.

Now comes a question that I don't wish to ask Mercy. I ask her, "Who comes back?" It is between you, the reader, and me. Given all the information that I have gotten from Mercy, it appears that a soul may have lived many times, occupying several different people. In that case, when God returns as Christ, are we reborn or are the souls reborn? If there is one soul for three people, who is reborn?

Both interviews with Mercy and my thoughts are included in the appendix.

Chapter 11
LIAM

I didn't know Liam's last name. Perhaps when I interviewed him I might find out. Liam was discovered by two of my guests who had come for a ghost communication lesson. Before the lesson they took a tour of Poquetanuck Cemetery #17. (I don't know why the number 17 is attached to the cemetery's name. It is the first village cemetery and dates back to the 1600s. I do know that Poquetanuck has belonged to three separate towns over the centuries. Perhaps it was the seventeenth cemetery in Groton.)

When everyone was assembled around the big table in the dining room, one of the guests said, "There is a grave in the old cemetery marked with the name 'Liam.' Have you ever communicated with him?" I hadn't. The guests were eager to see if the discovery of Liam's grave would lead to finding his spirit. It would be quite an accomplishment for them. When the session began, I made it a point to ask if there was a spirit named Liam in the house. The rods spread wide and a definite yes was seen by all. Everyone at the table was quite satisfied.

I welcomed Liam to our gathering and asked him if he would speak with us. He said yes. Then we started. It turns out that he was born and died in the eighteenth century. He was in his twenties when he passed away. During the session I passed the rods around the room. I noticed that Liam did not move the rods for any of the women. This is not unusual, since the rods work for very few people. They did work for two of the men. This was unusual. The spirits in the house don't like to communicate with men and very seldom do.

This dislike of men was caused by an accident that occurred in the 1700s. A young girl was pushed down the grand staircase by a man and died. I believe she may have been the daughter of a runaway slave. Several psychics who have visited have concurred that this is true. So currently only Liam and Mercy will communicate with the male guests.

Putting two and two together made me think that there was something about Liam that I was missing. So I asked him to point to a person at the table that he did not like. He pointed to a woman on my right. "Is there anyone else that you don't like?" He pointed to another woman.

Well, this is interesting, I thought. "Okay, Liam, would you please point to the person that you like the most at the table?" He pointed to a young man at the end of the table. "Hmm, are there any women at the table that you like?" Liam answered no. "How about the men. Do you dislike any of them?" Again, he answered no.

Here is how the conversation went for the next few minutes.

"Liam, did you ever spend time with a young lady when you were alive?"

"No."

"Did you like to spend time with men instead?"

"Yes."

"Did you fancy men in a sexual way?"

"Yes."

So there was the answer. Liam was gay. I was happy to hear this. It made the spirits of the house even more interesting. They were reflecting the very human aspects of who they were when they were alive.

Liam did one very scary thing to a guest who was staying at Captain Grant's. There was a production studio filming a show for a television series on finding historic artifacts. The cast had been with us for four days. In the morning one of the crew members came down to breakfast looking a little more than distraught. The rest of us, film crew included, were really curious and coaxed him to spill the beans. After a few minutes of being teased, he finally said okay and began to tell his tale of the night before.

"There was a ghost hovering over me in bed last night. He was stretched out right over the top of me, right there above me. Oh God, I couldn't move or scream or anything. I was terrified! I don't ever want to experience anything like that again. He was right above me looking down at me. I think he wanted sex or something. I'm not kidding you. It was scary as hell."

"Can you describe him?"

"Yes. He had dark hair and sideburns. The sideburns took an L-turn toward the bottom of the cheek. He had on a white shirt."

"He wasn't naked then?"

"No."

My guest was visibly shaken. In fact, he was shaking. It was his last day at the inn and I think he was grateful that the shooting was over. There had been other incidents while the film crew was at Captain Grant's, and they all believed that this man had had a ghostly experience. It was Liam, of course, just trying to get some attention from a man. He more than succeeded. I have also seen Liam, and he does have L-shaped sideburns and wears a long-sleeved white shirt and black pants.

Synopsis of My Interview with Liam

I started the conversation by asking questions regarding Liam being gay. I wanted to know how people treated him and what he thought of himself. I then attempted to learn what his last name was. I went through the alphabet trying to find out the first letter of his last name. He came up with a G. There are Geer family members in the back cemetery, so I asked if that was his name. He answered yes. With that response I went on to find out if Liam had had past lives, been married, or had children. It turns out that he had been a female once, but in none of his lives as either a man or a woman did he ever have children. I asked him if that was his task to allow him to ascend to heaven, and he answered in the affirmative.

Things seemed to be going well, so I decided to ask some questions about God. That is where the conversation didn't make any sense. I had the feeling that I might be experiencing some sort of game that Liam was playing. It seemed that a direct approach might work best, so I said, "Liam, are you teasing me?" The rods opened wide with a big yes. I ended the conversation at that point. Liam was unhappy and sent the rods spinning like helicopter blades.

Three days later I attempted another interview with Liam. I started by asking him if his last name was Geer. It was not. I then went back through the alphabet and he answered no to every letter. I began to think that he might be illiterate. When asked if he knew his letters, he said no. I discovered through several questions that Liam also had a learning disability. I brought Mercy into our conversation and was told by her that Liam was known as a kind soul but he was also called names and made fun of.

I felt sad for Liam. Perhaps in his new reincarnated life he will have more opportunities to learn and enjoy what he could not enjoy in his last life.

"I hope that when you are reborn you have a better life. And thank you for talking to me." With that I ended the interview, and I decided to explore the cemetery to see if I could find Liam's grave.

A month after my interview with Liam, I went to the cemetery. It was a beautiful October day and I thought there could be no time better to visit the old graveyard. The sky was a brilliant blue, the summer humidity was gone, and the sound of migrating birds filled the air. I took my time, savoring the fresh air and the honking geese overhead. The meadow was still a vibrant green and it felt as if all my senses were going to burst.

I hadn't been to the graveyard in a couple of months and was surprised to see how much vegetation had grown up over the summer. I started in the north end, making my way from grave to grave. My heart sank at the decay that was occurring on a yearly basis.

It took time to search. The headstones that were readable lay forward. If they were made of sandstone, they might be unreadable no matter how they lay. To check out a stone meant getting on the ground to read the name of the person who was buried there. Most of the stones were damaged beyond repair, their heartfelt inscriptions long gone. A few of the wealthier families of their time had marble or granite headstones that were still legible all of these years later.

I made my way to the south end of the graveyard and discovered that it was sliding down a deep slope. Some headstones were now tilted at an angle. The high stone wall at the south end was now only a couple of feet high. I knew in my heart that if I didn't make this known to someone, it would only continue to decay. I just didn't know who that someone was. I gathered my thoughts and decided to call city hall the following day, all to no avail. The town wasn't interested in the cemetery's upkeep.

As I rounded the southeast corner, the brush became difficult to maneuver. I found myself trying to step on the bases of plants to bend them over. I hadn't put on a jacket. In fact, I was in short sleeves. "How stupid," I thought. Finally about twenty feet later I was able to look again at gravestones. There were no readable stones where I had been that I could see. I searched each stone until I again approached the entrance. There were several Williams. With Liam being the end of that name, perhaps my guests hadn't read the entire headstone. If it was spelled in all capitals, which was likely, the end of William would look like LIAM. Could his name be William?

I decided that I should have another short talk with Liam. I returned to the bed and breakfast and got out my rods. With no one in the house, I figured the session would go well. I prepared myself and then called for Liam.

"Liam, this is Carol. Are you here?" The rods opened wide. "I've been out to the cemetery. I couldn't find a gravestone with the name Liam on it. Could your name be William?" Again the rods opened wide. "So you recognize the name William." The rods again opened up. "Should I call you William then?" Another yes answer appeared. "Okay, then was your last name Gallup?"

The rods flew open and shook. It was obvious that I had chosen the last name correctly. "William, there is a rather large stone in the cemetery with the name William Gallup. Could that be your father or grandfather?" William answered yes.

Finally, one mystery was solved.

I now rarely converse with Liam. I can't count on his answers being true, and not being able to see his face when we talk is a distinct disadvantage for me. I think of him as my innocent ghost, a naive and friendly spirit. Yet there is an exception to this assessment. Liam is very attracted to men, especially gay men. On occasion we have spirit events involving Liam. We recently hosted an event coordinator who specializes in ghost hunts. This coordinator and his team were on their way to the old cemetery when a couple of men in the group started feeling someone pat their behinds. The sensation of being patted went on throughout their visit to the gravesites. No one mentioned it to me until the next day. We were sitting at the breakfast table and I was talking about the different spirits that live in the home. I mentioned Liam and then added that he was gay. The room came alive with guests talking, several at once. "I was touched on my backside." "So was I." "I was too." "At first I thought it was my imagination, but then I got patted two more times." I said it must have been Liam. It would be just up his alley to do something like that.

I have talked quite a bit about the poor condition of the cemetery. We have a groundskeeper whom we have occasionally sent out to the cemetery to whack down the undergrowth. I called the Boy Scout troop in town, and they came and cleared out the trees and brush, but it all returned the next year. Then the cemetery commission spread vegetation killer all over the ground. That didn't work either.

The cemetery needs professional cemetery historians to put the stones back up, and the south end needs shoring up before caskets roll onto the ground and down into the stream and out to sea. It doesn't stay clean very long and would require yearly maintenance. I don't think that will ever happen.

Chapter 12
PETE

Pete was also discovered by guests. A paranormal investigative team consisting of a husband and wife got an EVP of other spirits talking about Pete. They had hooked up an EVP in the basement and got one of their best recordings. This EVP was longer than normal. Most of them are quite short, being just one or two words. This is what was said: "Pete's over there. He's trouble."

I was surprised to discover that some of the house's spirits thought that one of them was "trouble." I wondered whether I should talk with this spirit or not. I don't want any evil to fall upon Captain Grant's, and I'm am always careful not to call upon any spirit that may be so inclined.

I didn't have to wait long. About a week later, during a communication session, I encountered Pete. At the start of each session I find out if the spirit is male or female, young or adult, and then begin to ask names. During this session, I went through all of the male names that I had previously talked to and kept getting a no answer.

I thought that perhaps this Pete fellow was going to attempt to talk with a live person. When I asked if it was Pete, the answer was yes.

I wanted to learn something about Pete and decided to attempt to communicate with him at a later time. One of the questions that I have asked all the spirits is "Would you rather be alive than in the world you are in now?" In my interview with Pete, his answer to this question was yes. He is the only spirit at Captain Grant's that wants to be reborn. In fact, he is the only spirit that I have ever talked to that wants to be reborn. I asked him if he could go to the light and he said no. Knowing what the EVP had said, I decided to ask him about his personal character when he was alive.

"Pete, when you were alive did you do things that you need to atone for?"

"Yes."

"Is that keeping you from going to the light?"

"Yes."

"You want another chance to live your life as a better person?"

"Yes."

From what I learned from Mercy, I think Pete is going to get that chance. If he was evil, according to Mercy, when he died his soul would have also died—unless there is a purgatory and he's stuck there for eternity. I will have to find out if that is a possibility.

Synopsis of My Interview with Pete

When I start the interview with Pete, I want to get some general knowledge of his former life. After going through the centuries, I learn that he is currently the oldest spirit in the house, having died in the 1600s. Even though that is when he died, he didn't move into the Grant home until the 1900s. I don't know where his spirit was from the time of his death until his appearance at Captain Grant's.

It turns out that Pete has had four lives, the first one as a Hebrew in the first century. His reincarnations have taken longer than those of anyone I have previously conversed with, given an average of about five hundred years each.

I also want to explore why he is "trouble." As it turns out, in three of his lives he murdered someone. He was a thief and generally not a good person.

At the end of my session with Pete, I say: "Pete, I am alive. Supposedly I have had other lives. I don't remember them or what I did wrong. When I came into this life it was as if I was a new soul. There was nothing to keep me from making the same mistakes again. When you are reborn are you going to kill again?"

Silence. The rods don't move.

I'm exhausted. I have one spirit interview left and I feel completely drained.

During my interview with Pete, I learned that his last name was Ledyard, so when I get back to my office, I decide to look up this family name. I want to explore what Pete said to verify his story. I don't have any success. The Ledyards arrived in the Colonies after the date that Pete described. He claimed to have been born prior to the family arriving in Groton. I decide to let the information rest. I also need a respite and plan to hold off on the next spirit communication session for a couple of days.

Chapter 13
THE VICTIM

When I purchased the Avery house that I now live in, I knew someone had been murdered in it. I don't know how I knew, I just knew. I was thirty-nine years old and did not know how to communicate with the spirits, but I was intuitive. I believe that my intuition is driven by an ability to observe what others may miss. I don't believe that it is some magical gift, but a gathering of information into a logical conclusion.

When I bought the Avery house, it was cut into two living areas. One part was about one quarter of the house. To get to this part, you needed to climb an outside staircase that the town condemned right after I bought the house. The small area was cold and I didn't use it in the winter. There were no laundry facilities, so laundry had to be carried down the backstairs, which were dangerous to descend. To access the main part of the house, you needed to go down those same stairs and enter through the back door. The space was called a mother-in-law apartment by the people from whom I bought the house. This being the case, it would have been even more difficult for an elderly person to come and go. I believed that little regard was paid to the person living in this small space. I wondered if my intuition about someone being murdered didn't have something to do with this space.

I also wondered if there might be a ghost in the house. Maybe it could be the person whom I suspected might have been murdered. I didn't give it a lot of thought at the time. It was futile to speculate on the matter because I had no way of contacting the spirit world.

In 1988, two years after buying the home, I had a horrific ghostly experience. My partner, who usually stayed awake until 2:00 a.m., was asleep by 10:00 p.m. that night. This was an unlikely occurrence. He started to snore and I began to read my Bible. Then I felt something creep up my legs until I was completely overtaken. I tried to scream but couldn't. When I tried to move my arms, nothing would happen. I tried to open my mouth to scream. I tried to move in any way possible in order to awaken my partner, but I couldn't do that either. I am quite a rational thinker and I sat still and thought, "I need to surprise this entity and use all of my strength and scream." I closed my eyes and concentrated. Then I let out a dreadful scream.

My partner awoke. He sat up in bed and just stared at me. "What happened? Why did you scream?" All I could do was sob. I sobbed for a long, long time.

The next day I told a friend of mine, who was a born-again Christian, about the incident. I wanted to do an exorcism and was afraid to call a priest. (I didn't want to be called nuts.) She discouraged me and said that it could be very dangerous. But I was my usual self, undaunted. She gave me some literature and asked me to make a promise that I would read all of it. I agreed.

After about a week or two of studying, I decided that I was ready. I asked God for protection and went into my keeping room to perform the ritual. I had my Bible, a cross, my prayer book, holy water, and whatever else I was supposed to have. I prayed like I had never prayed before. I demanded that the spirit leave my home in the name of Jesus Christ.

About an hour passed while I prayed and continued to demand that the spirit leave. Then the atmospheric pressure in the house changed. It was as if a great wind came from the dining room into the keeping room and then straight up through the house. The exorcism was successful. When the spirit left, the air in the house felt light. I thought, "I can float." Of course I couldn't, but I did kneel and thank God that the spirit was gone.

The spirit at the back door, which I photographed in the Avery house in August 1986. Photo credit: author

This spirit entered the home where the back door was in 1790. In 1817 an addition was built, so the back door is now twenty feet farther back. When I bought the home in 1986, I captured this spirit on my camera twice, both times at the original back door.

In 2014 I began to do short spirit sessions using my L-rods. I would ask a couple of questions and then put the rods away. There was a female spirit that always answered. Eventually I asked her if she had been murdered in the upstairs part of the home that was added in 1817. The rods opened wide with an affirmative answer. Only if the spirit that I had banned from the home was still alive after 1817 could he be the murderer. If he had been alive past 1817, why hadn't he used the new doorway? I decided to interview the female spirit and attempt to find the answers to my questions.

Synopsis of My Interview with the Victim

I performed this interview in an upstairs bedroom that my husband and I had turned into an office. I also confirmed that this was the same woman who had been responding to me before. She was. She had lived and died in the home, smothered by a family member. I thought, "Who am I to judge this happening?" The woman was quite old and apparently ill. Perhaps it may have been a mercy killing. I did not go into dates when this occurred and I thought it wise to avoid too many details. In the end she told me that she just wanted someone to know what had really happened. She voiced no animosity toward anyone.

I would never go to the police. They would think that I'm as crazy as they get. Then I thought, "It doesn't matter anymore. They are all dead. And she is at peace."

I have been asked many times by my guests if anyone has died in the Grant or the Avery home. I always say yes. The homes in this historic village are old, mostly from the seventeenth and early eighteenth century. Most of the colonial population died at home. There were no funeral homes. The dead were laid out at home in the parlor. This custom continued into the 1950s. Keeping rooms became parlors, and in the mid-1900s parlors became living rooms. (The term *parlor* is now used primarily for funeral parlors.)

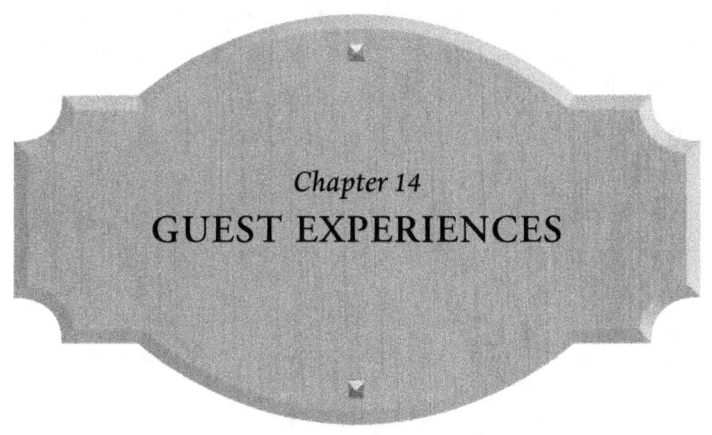

Chapter 14
GUEST EXPERIENCES

The next four chapters contain accounts of experiences that guests have had at Captain Grant's and have written about in diaries from January 19, 2009, up until June 2016. Four of our bedrooms have a leather-bound book of lined pages in which our guests, if they choose, can share something about their stay with future guests. These are only samplings of some of the experiences. Also, of the notes that I chose to include here, there are only excerpts and not the full notes. The writing style is close to what the guests actually wrote. Most notes were probably written hastily and reflect that in the word usage and spelling. My comments are in parentheses at the end. I also have ideas about the spirits that guests have mentioned and who they might be.

I believe that the giggling child in Captain Grant's is Deborah Adams. There are also two other children that I know of, a boy named John who died in the 1900s and the daughter of a runaway slave who died in the 1800s prior to the Civil War. My guess is that these children are also responsible for the rolling balls in the attic.

The walking in the attic is probably Daniel. He is also the spirit that the children from *Psychic Kids* told to leave the house.

Mercy Adelaide Grant is a most loving spirit and might be responsible for touches that guests experience. The pats on the face occur most often in the Adelaide and Collette bedrooms.

Pats on men's private places are probably caused by Liam.

You will read more excerpts in some rooms than in others. This is because some rooms are more haunted than others.

Chapter 15
ADELAIDE ROOM

In this room the back window looks directly over the lawn and into the old cemetery. A massive hand-hewn beam crosses the ceiling. The furniture is authentic early nineteenth century. It is like stepping back in time when you walk through the door and is probably why this is the most haunted room in the house.

When I purchased the house, it had only one bathroom for all four bedrooms on the second floor. I cut that overly large bathroom in half, making one half go to the Adelaide room and the other half to the Collette room. I have said that Adelaide is the most haunted room in the house, but it is actually the Adelaide bathroom where all the action takes place. The Collette headboard is on the other side of that bathroom wall. Moans and whispering coming from that wall have been heard by guests sleeping in Collette. The general feeling of the room is one of warmth and love. Being cared for is also a way to explain it. When you read the notes that I am sharing with you here, you will see some similarities but also many differences in our guests' experiences. It's as if the spirits are individualizing their visits to accommodate our guests.

Now for the shared writings of our guests. This room's diary is filled with drawings and experiences.

The Adelaide room in Captain Grant's. Photo credit: Bruce Peter Morin

11/5/10

Dear Ted and Carol,

Though we did not see a ghost nor catch anything on audio we did snap a picture of an orb. A few unexplained things such as around 9:30. No one was here but my husband and myself when we heard the front door open and someone walking up the stairs. Our bedroom door was opened so I got up to shut it and to my amazement there was no one in the hall or in the house. Another thing was my husband went nuts looking for his medication, emptying the entire cosmetic bag to no avail. In the morning his meds were on top of the bag he searched. No answer for this!

—Couple on a short get away.

(Carol: It is a common occurrence for items to disappear and then reappear at a later time in another place. This is one of the happenings that drive all of us here a little crazy.)

11/6/10

This room is beautiful. We took lots of pictures. So far, many orbs to report but we may see more once we view on the laptop. My husband heard someone go out the deck & then a shadow go downstairs—but no footsteps. What a great getaway.

—Couple from New York

(Carol: It would be nearly impossible to walk in this home unheard. With every step there is a creak.)

2/19/2011

Adelaide came by to visit. Rattling our door knob, knocking on the wall & my husband said something was tickling his ear in the middle of the night (& it wasn't me). We will add it to our list of first experiences.

—Retired couple from New Jersey

2/20/11

I wasn't expecting anything along the lines of paranormal, but when my friend and I noticed the shower curtain rings pulled off the shower rod—and we were the only ones in the room at the time—I can only say there is no explanation. And I am glad to have had an encounter with the unknown. Thank you.

—Paralegal from New Jersey

(Carol: When Tadashi glued and screwed the shower curtain rod to the wall, the rings then started being lifted off the rod. This always happens at night.)

3/19/11

My friend and I have been here only 15 hours and I am already SO THRILLED with all of our experiences.

1. Went out to dinner last night, came back at 11:30 & a ball that I brought was not where I left it. I left it on the dresser & it was on the middle of the bed when we came back.
2. Got a peek up in the attic & took pics I got 3 great pics of really bright perfectly round orbs.
3. As I'm writing this, my friend & I both just heard a "ting" & we were like, what the heck was that? Mind you it's 10:30 AM. So I took this pen & tapped on the lamp & parts of the sconce on the wall & found that the base/circle part of the sconce made the same "ting" when I tapped it. COOL!
4. Around 3:30/4 AM footsteps in the hall, but no doors opening or closing.
5. I heard a little girl giggling around 4 am down the hall. My friend didn't hear it though. But at breakfast just now, our neighbor across the hall said she heard it & assumed kids were staying here. No kids here.
6. Don't know when it moved, but discovered one of my daughter's stuffed animals under my pillow when we woke up. That kinda freaked me out I'll be honest. But at the same time I'm so intrigued.

I just feel the need to say that I'm not a freak making this stuff up. I'm a soon-to-be 40 married mother of 2 kids. I'm still blown away that all of this happened. Oh & this morning during breakfast, Carol was about to get out the divining rods for us & I ran up here to get my camera. Mind you I had our key & locked the door. We were downstairs for maybe 45 minutes and when I ran up here the door was open by 1 foot. Nobody had been up here. The stairs/floors are loud—we would have known. Woke up a few times last night. Loud footsteps @3 AM. Ball rolling. Possibly a toy w/ wheels rolling. WOW. I'm ready to go home. Thanks for an amazing experience.

—Norwalk, Connecticut

7/8/11

Last night I was touched twice while sleeping. A nudge in my back and someone stroking my hand. My cousin heard someone screaming her name and also a dinner bell—both while she was in the shower. We were honored to be acknowledged by our paranormal hosts.

—Two sisters

(Carol: I and others have had the same experience of hearing someone loudly call out our names.)

7/20/11

Lovely stay with family. Quiet for the first two nights, peaceful. Then 3rd night. Heard loud crashes in the night. Woke up to find shower curtain laying across the entire bathroom. Very difficult to find out how it got there. Still felt safe and fun. I could feel the positive energy in the room, waiting to be acknowledged. What a great vacation.

—Family reunion guests

8/17/11

Last night we left bathroom door ajar at 11 pm. At 2 am door was closed. The door doesn't swing so easy in that direction. Also my wife heard a child's giggle around 4 am. We were the only guests in the house. Maybe it was the sherry.

—Astoria, New York

8/26/11

Yes, we are believers! When we heard the noise above us, like children rolling a ball back and forth, it was AWESOME. We are already planning a trip back in October.

—Vermonters

9/16/11

Romantic weekend getaway for my boyfriend and I. He is so fascinated by all things ghostly. I am a solid sensible NH woman. I went up to the 3rd floor balcony to see what I could spot. Looking down at the road I heard a woman's voice not 2 feet from my left side. I could not make out her words but the voice sounded like it was on the other side of glass in the attic. There was no one in the attic. My boyfriend was coming up the stairs to join me on the balcony and swears he did not speak since coming outside and there was only one other couple over in the Holly room (Carol: The Holly room is in the home next door.) On his last visit, 6 years ago he was with a woman whose face turned white as a sheet when a chess piece levitated and dropped to the floor. Same chess piece that had been knocked to the floor and John and other guests that weekend kept picking up and putting back on chessboard in parlor.

—New Hampshire couple.

(Carol: This happened in the East Keeping room. It was the king. I still have him as a memento. Since the home was built by colonists from Scotland, just maybe they were trying to make a statement about King George II.)

2/5/2012

We were sitting on the bed when my husband saw a light near the bathroom door so he took his camera and start recording this spot and out of nowhere this orb starts going all over going in different directions up and down. It was cool. I'm not into this stuff but for some reason I was not scared and had a very restful sleep until somewhere in the middle of the night I hear something like a conversation but more like a murmur but my husband's snoring didn't let me grab where it was coming from.

—Winter guests

4/20/12

The three of us took a walk out to the cemetery in the back where caught some interesting video of a particular bright orange orb that was following us, and stayed perfectly still in the center of the lens frame as we did our opening prayers. In particular we also caught a photograph of another glowing orb upon 50X zoom it resembles a woman looking down at her very pregnant belly (no arms or legs)... interesting part is... in the next frame the orb splits into two, a tiny orb and a larger orb.

In our room, we did have the small table near the bathroom appear to move 5–6" away from the wall although we did not see it move ourselves. We will be back and maybe stay in the Collette room then. Happy Ghost Hunting.

—Happy Ghost Hunters

(Carol: I have seen this orb in the cemetery many times with my naked eye. So have my neighbors. It is sometimes orange and other times bright red. There is nothing beyond the cemetery, only land and trees. I have never gone out to the cemetery in the dark, even when I see the light. I'm not sure why, except that my instincts tell me not to venture out there at night. As for the little table by the bathroom door, it has to weigh at least sixty pounds. It has a marble top. It has never moved since.)

5/6/12

This is our third time staying here and we just love it. It is so peaceful and beautiful. Our second night here in the Adelaide room I heard noises like someone was dragging furniture across the floor. This lasted 3–4 minutes. I went to the attic to see if anything was moved and all was exactly as it was the day before when we saw it.

—A couple

7/10/12

Our stay was very interesting to say the least. Around 10 pm seeing how we had the entire place to ourselves, my husband and I sat at the top of the stairs and started some EVP recording. I had just put on our night vision goggles when a bat flew towards my face and into the sitting area!

Very cute little bat my husband later caught it in a blanket and released it outside. We stayed up past 3 AM hoping to encounter something but the house was very quiet and still. I suggested we go to bed. We had just fallen to sleep, no more than 10 minutes in and our door handle shook vigorously as if someone frantically trying to get in. I wake up my husband sits up in bed and I asked him, "Did you hear that?" He says yes and goes to see if it was kids playing games. No one was there. We now know not to lock the door when we visit here again.

—A couple

(Carol: The blanket has since been cleaned. It is free of anything bat. Just a note about bats: When released, they often find their way back in. They also eat all our nighttime bugs. No mosquitoes at Captain Grant's.)

12/11/12

Breakfast was fantastic!! I had a great time staying here. I did hear a child talking in the hallway and a few other noises during the night. P.S. Just finished taking shower. While in shower toilet flushed, my wife wasn't in there she was packing.

—Guests' first experience at a bed and breakfast

(Carol: Our toilets can't flush themselves.)

2/24/13

Our first night, we heard footsteps in the attic and the sounds of furniture being moved across the floor. We heard what sounded like something rolling down the hallway.

It was so much fun to hear the stories of other guests at breakfast. We really enjoyed the paranormal team that was here at the same time as us. We had a great time following them and participating in their investigation.

—Massachusetts couple

4/19/13

The first night in the Adelaide room I heard giggling at 2:00 AM but thought it was our neighbors. It wasn't!!! Apparently it was the 5 year old Debra Adams. Many times that night we heard people moving around (or so we thought). No one was up and about. The second night was quiet.

—Minnesota travelers

10/8/13

I rarely sign my name in guest books but this was one of the strangest experiences I have ever had! First let me say that I have always been a skeptic regarding the paranormal until my four nights in the Adelaide room. The first night. Nothing.

The second night I lived a decade of vivid dreams, more dreams than I have experienced in my life and they were so lifelike. I woke hoping some were reality while praying others were not...

The third night more vivid dreams. The last one erotic & vivid. I was with one of my best friend's stunning wife in the bed and at first all was exciting until I realized (or thought twice about) I could not do this to my best friend. I tried to get her off me because I knew what I was doing was wrong. She resisted me while trying to get her off the top of me. I pushed harder struggling with her and as I awoke pushing her off of me and sitting up in the bed I saw a sight that will haunt me forever in more ways than one! I opened my eyes to see a man in white with thick bushy dark side burns is what I had been struggling with! Being 100% straight I was a bit embarrassed regarding this but felt the need to tell this.

I never wanted or cared about the paranormal but am now totally intrigued by it and want to learn/see/experience more.

—Actor New York City

(Carol: I believe this spirit was Liam.)

2/13/15

It was a short notice decision to get away for a couple days and we were lucky to find this online. Since the Adelaide room has a reputation we made sure to ask for it. We were alone for both nights. Nothing happened the first night and I so hoped it would. However, the next night when my husband turned the kitchen light off he heard a knocking. Very quick and he swears it was imagined. Around 10:30 pm I heard muffled talking somewhere by the bathroom but didn't think much of it. When we settled in for sleep at 11:45 pm I still heard the talking. Thinking a radio or TV was left on, my husband and I walked through the whole house trying to find it. Couldn't find anything. Came back to the room and continued to hear it till I fell asleep. Woke up at 2 am and 4 am and the noises were gone.

—Enfield, Connecticut

(Carol: I have had this same experience. It is so frustrating not to be able to find the source of the talking. Just as soon as you think you are approaching the source, the talking stops.)

9/14/15

Videoed on my phone 2 hrs. of bright orbs flying around the Adelaide room from the moment we turned out the lights—the naked eye couldn't see much—but w/ the phone on the video on in the room in the dark, the orbs were lights everywhere—gold & white flying every which way straight at us—sending the inn the footage—only caught on still camera foggy areas—but the live videos are like watching shooting stars—they seemed to respond to my voice—I asked them to slow down—be bigger—and they did—it was amazing!!!!!! I love it here.

—Young couple from New York

1/17/16

We explored in an undisclosed place by which clearly heard a woman breathing on our right side. We bolted down the stairs to do an EVP session w/ Mercy Adelaide. Results were not only orbs unlikely to be dust but a flash of light also occurred within the dining area that bolted from right to left. We then went to the game room to collect our thoughts while being alarmed by the loud & swift footsteps down below while calling out & looking to only get no response back.

—Returnees from Connecticut

(Carol: The flash of light in the dining room has also occurred during breakfast with a table full of guests.)

Chapter 16
COLLETTE ROOM

The Collette room is in the back of the house and also faces the back lawn and the old cemetery. In the winter months you can see monuments over the stone wall. In the summer the cemetery is obscured by trees and vines. The two back bedrooms have a massive hand-hewn beam that runs through the middle of their ceilings. The floor in the Collette room is original to the house and is 262 years old. In fact, all of the wooden structure of the house is authentic.

When I purchased the house, this was the room where we had the most spirit encounters. It now ranks second in paranormal phenomena. The room has a queen sleigh bed and an iron day bed. In the queen bed, guests hear moans from the Adelaide bathroom (which wasn't there until fifty years ago). Most of the brushings of cheeks and other occurrences happen to the person sleeping in the day bed. When I started the renovations, this was the largest room in the home. I ended up running a hallway down one side of the room, taking out almost three feet of width, and it is still the largest bedroom. It is also the most masculine bedroom that we have for guests.

Now, enjoy what guests have written in the Collette diary.

The Collette room in Captain Grant's. Photo credit: Bruce Peter Morin

11/22/11

Hi Ted and Carol.

This is a beautiful home. It is naturally very peaceful. To be in a home with so much history & charm is so wonderful! It was really awesome to find that cemetery in the back. You guys really do a great job of making everyone feel like we are welcomed and in a different time.

P.S. We will try to upload our ghost communication class & orb on you tube. The class was so incredible! Debra is really a special little girl—I know in my heart that she must have been a guide for our grandfather to able to communicate with us today.

—A couple from somewhere in New England

(Carol: Debra is Deborah Adams, who died of illness in the 1700s. She was five years old when she perished.)

3/19/12

Good morning! Well to say the least, this has been by far the most interesting night my wife and I have ever spent. First I would like to state that I have never encountered any experiences like tonight.

My wife saw an orb fly across the room: I heard strange drumming noises near the window on 2 occasions (coincidentally, I read my little girl a story earlier on the balcony and addressed the "occupants" if they could drum...)

While I was about to doze off I heard a loud voice say a sound—which now occurs to me to sound like her name. My four year old does not talk in her sleep and was not restless upon investigating. We have other murmurs to such an extent that we deem it necessary to vacate immediately. Your house is beautiful and it was a real pleasure staying but alas we must depart.

—A young family of three

2/27/12

We hope to come again soon. We did experience unseen visitors—and that was very interesting. Doors opening, footsteps—WOW.

—A young couple from Greenfield, Massachusetts

4/18/12

P.S. Heard some banging while asleep on first evening. Awake to some movements on side of bed. Quite scary, but exciting too! We had a blast and will return.

—A couple from Blandford, Massachusetts

5/9/12

The first night I woke up suddenly, feeling as if someone was standing next to the bed only to find my shoes had been moved. Also, my phone was dead—after being on the charger all night. We went for a walk returned to our room I smelled perfume. I was not wearing perfume.

Night #2—I awoke to someone breathing in my ear and other incidents that I haven't the time to write about—to sum it up, it was a great paranormal experience! We got some great photos of orbs as well! P.S. Daniel made his presence very well known around midnight-ish as he stomped through the parlor while we were quietly sitting.

—Two sisters and their mother

(Carol: None of our staff wear perfume, because I am allergic to most brands.)

6/15/12

I never believed in spirits until...

Until we stayed here this book that I am writing in was not the journal that was in our room that we read together. We went out for the evening, returned and interestingly enough the journal that was in our room was not when we returned but the one I'm writing in was and 2 pillows were on the floor when we returned, the next morning we woke up got ready for breakfast. Came back to our room the door was shut and locked when we left when we came back upstairs. The door was open wide open. We went for a walk returned to our room I smelled perfume When we entered I was not wearing perfume... Strange, unexplainable, but never did we feel like we had to leave in a hurry. We will stay again.

—Massachusetts residents

8/31/12

I wanted you and anyone else reading this that I believe that there is the spirit of a little boy named John here. He was most able to communicate through the dowsing rods which he was quite adept at. He followed us around most of the night & we had a lot of fun with him So to anyone else who comes here and reads this—if you contact John, please tell him Mary says hello!

—North Attleboro, Massachusetts

11/5/12

We had one experience while in this room. While showering we heard a knocking on the shower wall 3 times. Upon investigating the room down the hall, we found no one there. Just an empty room. We used dowsing meters and EVP meters with no results.

—Bay Shore, New York

(Carol: The room down the hall is the Adelaide room.)

2/23/13

Some light play disturbances in the Collette room. When we check in the room next us "Amy" room my sister & I heard laughing child. My friend opened door stating no one was in there. Had quite a few experiences all related to the Amy Room.

—Two women from Massachusetts

4/28/13
No visits from friends but my phone lit up during the night saying I had a voicemail only to find there was none. Never did that before.

—A young couple from Rehoboth, Massachusetts

8/20/13 FULL BLUE MOON
It's about 11:45 and I plugged in our phones. My phone started going crazy a few seconds later as if someone was dialing very fast. We fell asleep. About 1:30 in the morning the phone started acting erratic again. It was making a sound like when the old phones were left off the hook and you get the dial tone that keeps going off. It did this for about 1 min. We were awoken again 2 hours later. Same sound but longer the second time. We jumped out of bed. As there was no explanation for this to happen. The phone I had put on silent when I plugged it in to charge.

Happy Haunting

—A couple from New York

3/30/14
At 2:38 am the covers were pulled off of me. My partner told me it was him! He fessed up in the morning. He only said that to me so I would go back to sleep and proceeded to tell the covers were pulled off of him a few times.

—A young couple in love

(Carol: This only happens in the Collette and Amy rooms.)

10/18/14

2nd time for us—We live approx. an hour away. Wonderful location to both casinos.

Added bonus (at least to us) that this is a haunted B&B. Had a "experience" our 1st night here this time or our 2nd night on this stay. I experienced a little girl on the right side of my bed. Very brief. We will be back.

—Married couple

11/1/14

This is our 2nd time here. The last time we were here we picked up some voices on the voice recorder in the cemetery. This time we received a few experiences in the attic with the evp 11 meter & dousing rods. In the Collette Room we received the same with a little more activity & also some voices on the recorder, which we don't know exactly what they are saying but they happened where my husband was in the room alone. The breakfast was great as usual & the conversation was very interesting.

—Three ghost-hunting friends

3/22/15

We had an awesome experience here!! Lots of paranormal things going on throughout the middle of the night. Aside from the strange noises, my husband felt pokes all night and around 4:00AM, he woke up screaming!! Freaked me out that's for sure!! A weird mist of smoke covered the shaky window. We definitely felt something or someone in our room with us.

—Love from a great couple

5/29/15

Our first stay here @ Captain Grant's and must say the room and atmosphere was most pleasant. Loved the décor & house, being a furniture & architectural woodworker, I loved the way things are restored & cared for. My wife & I weren't in the Collette room 5 minutes when we heard a "yahoo" softly in a woman's voice. At which time we turned to face each other simultaneously & said "what." We both came to the immediate conclusion it was neither of us. We smiled a knowing smile & went on unpacking for our stay. "FYI"—there were no other guests in the house @ this time. Awakened @ 2:30 A.M., by what I can only describe as a pressure around my body. Ma was still asleep. Saw just outside the window a misty form. Was it night fog or something else. Lasted less than a minute. Undisturbed the rest of the night.

—Unknown guests

7/24/15

Thank you so much for your wonderful hospitality. Our haunted experiences are pretty amazing. Went to the old cemetery out in the woods in the back of the house. Pretty creepy! Our sister captured a lot of mist in one of the pictures. I did have a couple of experiences while here. The first night I felt someone pulling the covers off of me. Didn't get much sleep that night. After this happened to me I read in this book how someone else had the same experience as me. This blew me away! Also someone wrote about a pillow ending up on the floor. Well that happened to me too. Heard some creaks & then heard a women's voice right by the door. This was about 2:30 in the morning. Freaked me out that I had to turn on the T.V. right away. I really didn't want to fear anything. This stay was wonderful. Thank you. It was so peaceful sitting out in the yard in the gazebo. Wish we could've had a bonfire but it was raining. Oh well. I was sitting in the living room with my dog. He started staring at the blue chair in the corner. Kept looking it up and down and then started to growl a little. I believe he did see a spirit. I feel someone else was around.

God Bless & hope to see you both again.

—A couple from North Easton, Massachusetts

(No date)
ALL I HAVE TO SAY IS GOOD LUCK SLEEPING.
—SAS

10/9/15
Our stay was terrific! We enjoyed the cozy room and all of the amenities. We had an eventful night consisting of a cool breeze blow (windows shut). A picture we took of the children's painting depicts a figure in our photo, dragging of chains were heard in the early morning as well as a recording I captured of a voice saying "what" when we were downstairs. Thank you for a great experience!!

P.S. Faint tapping of drums.

—From Newark, Delaware

11/8/15
Jeremiah 29:11
For I know the plans I have for you, declares the Lord. Plans to prosper you and never harm you, plans to give you hope and a great future. All our love.

1/10/16

As skeptical as I might be, you, Carol, appeared in my dream telling me to "wake up." Which I kept asking "What Happened!" I woke up frightened and within a few minutes I felt a presence and started to levitate over my granddaughter and husband, mumbling and unable to speak. The experience was so real. I closed my eyes, but was not sleeping, when I saw a bright, white light in a window in which appeared a man in dark clothes, followed by an image of a girl in white. My granddaughter, who was sleeping next to me as I continued to see spirits in white and a man in dark clothes, would squeeze my arm gently as if to keep me focused on all I was seeing; Clouds, beautiful trees and clear visions of small and larger spirits. I checked the time after my first encounter and it was 4:45 and this continued until 7:30. When I stopped focusing on the images and they began to weaken. P.S. I also, for a second time, rose above our bed and actually saw my husband, the wee one and myself in a white light, sleeping—so real!

—Grandparents and their granddaughter

(Carol: What this woman experienced was an out-of-body experience. I experienced that same type of event when I was eight years old.)

Chapter 17
ELIZABETH ROOM

The Elizabeth room is one of two rooms facing the front lawn and the cemetery across the street. It is also next to the upper deck, which is an outdoor living room. This room did not have the same level of activity that the Adelaide and Collette rooms had up until September of 2015, when the spirits began to gather. (I write about this in chapter 21, "The Gathering.") Now things seem to be happening on a regular basis.

From the beginning of Captain Grant's, the Elizabeth room has been the favorite of guests. It is a bit smaller than the other rooms, but that doesn't seem to matter. It has a four-poster canopy cherry bed that my husband handcrafted. The one comment that we repeatedly get from guests is, "We were so comfortable. It felt like home." I have heard that comment hundreds of times. I believe that the spirits in the home take care of our guests. The spirits have told me, in our conversations, that they like having guests in the home.

128 Chapter 17

The Elizabeth room in Captain Grant's. Photo credit: Bruce Peter Morin

Up until 2012, the only experiences recorded by guests in the Elizabeth room were sounds they would hear coming from the hallway. After September 2015, some of the most unusual happenings occurred in this room. They were not recorded in the room's diary.

Now enjoy the telling of the stories in this room.

> 4/28/10
>
> Thanks Ted and Carol
>
> We had an incredible time looking for ghosts! Caught the voices of what sounded like a small child singing outside this room. We'll let you know anything else we find when we review the tapes.
>
> —Ghost Hunters

(Carol: Many of our guests in the Elizabeth and Adelaide rooms have heard this child. It is a girl and I suspect that it is Deborah Adams.)

1/15/12
We did have one encounter—My wife & I both clearly heard the voice of a young child say, "Ma." No one was around.
—Cranston, Rhode Island

2/22/12
I had a amazing stay at this B&B. I heard a little girl's voice laughing in our room and footsteps in the night. Be back soon.
—Rhode Island

3/20/12
I admit I am a bit of a skeptic but open minded so I decided to record an experience on the last night of our stay. Let reader be the judge or interpreter of the happening. Not much really, just a poke in the nose.

At 1:30 am I was in half sleep after about 3 hours of sound sleep. Lying on my back, my wife asleep and facing the opposite wall. My arms and hands were under the covers, when I felt 3 taps on the nose. On my left nostril hard enough to close the nostril but soft enough not to move my head. If only once, I may have dismissed it but 3 times brought an awareness not to be denied because I was fully awake by the second tap. No sounds were heard. I got up and looked around the room and all was quiet. At times I do hold my breath in my sleep but I have never felt anything like this sensation. It was what it was. Did a ghost save my life?

—Newington, Connecticut

5/25/12

We enjoyed every second being here. We were thrilled to have some personal experiences with the spirits of Captain Grant's 1754 as well. It was quite thrilling to be the only guests in the house for the last few nights, making the unexplained noise, well, unexplained. We did hear walking about above us in the early morning. I heard the name Sarah spoken to me outside on my way to the cemetery. Our biggest thrill was in the game room last night where it was very cold when the rest of the house was hot and both heard a woman's voice at the same time.

—Highland Lakes, New York

(Carol: The game room has a separate heating system, so that might have caused the temperature difference. The name Sarah has been mentioned to me several times by guests, but I have yet to have a conversation with her. The walking in the attic occurs around 4:00 to 5:00 a.m., though that can vary some. At one time this male spirit's voice was heard only in the Adelaide room, but now it is heard in all second-floor rooms. I believe this spirit is Daniel.)

11/25/12

We loved our room & the great breakfast. Our experiences in our room were a knock & jiggle of the door handle yet no one was in the hall ... Seems like the ghosts are friendly yet mischievous.

—A family of five

(Carol: This is where I want to point out the time separation of sightings in this room. The previous sighting was on November 25, 2012, and the next one was on November 27, 2015.)

11/27/15

The midnight walk through the cemetery in the back was fascinating and spooky. We heard footsteps in the hall our last night here! Thought we saw people in our room at night! And even had a vitamin move on a table when our back was turned. Yikes!!

—A newly married couple

Chapter 18
AMY ROOM

The Amy room also overlooks the front lawn and the cemetery across the street. When I purchased the home, this room had no means of heat. It also had only one light socket. I was told by the real estate agent that the owners didn't want any heat in their room, but that didn't quite explain why the room felt so abandoned. (It is possible that someone may have died in that room.) It does have a chimney running through its walls, so the lack of heating was intentional.

As I recounted earlier, in the early 1900s two sisters inherited the home. One was going to be married and the other slept with her sister's intended husband. They became famous in town for their hatred of each other. They both continued to live in the house but attempted to cut it in half. They cut a channel through the building and took out all of the original fireplaces and put in two heating systems. One of the furnaces installed in 1916 was still there at the time of my purchase. This particular room, Amy, seems to have been neglected during that time period. Perhaps the hatred of the sisters kept the spirits away. It is now a bright and sunny room, complete with a gas fireplace. It is a welcoming room but is the least active of all the rooms in terms of spirits.

The first diary entry is dated March 14, 2009. The first reported haunting by a guest was on November 6, 2010.

The Amy room in Captain Grant's. Photo credit: Bruce Peter Morin

11/6/2010

Dear Ted and Carol,

We returned @ 11:00 P.M. Everyone seemed to be retired for the night. Watched a little T.V. then went to sleep... Around 1:00 pm I heard footsteps above me. (I had heard someone earlier in their room) so these steps were definitely over my head) I tapped my husband so he could hear. I counted 5 steps... That was it. Quiet for remainder of the night. We will be back.

—A young couple

11/20/10

Beautiful and relaxing as ever. Had a 2nd encounter in the Adelaide room. Someone threw a bar of soap at me & it struck my ankle with such force, I was rattled. The first encounter was a woman staring out of the window & she turned to look at me with a smile on her face.

—Repeat guests

(Carol: Even though this entry is written in the Amy diary, it appears that the guest had also explored the Adelaide room. Also, if you note the dates between this encounter and the next one, you will see how seldom experiences occur in this room.)

4/3/12

We loved our stay here. From the breakfast to the spirit Mercy freaking out my wife because she has a crush on my beard, this whole experience has been great.

—Artist from New England

(Carol: I did a ghost communication lesson in the dining room that morning and contacted Mercy. When I asked her if she liked anyone in particular, she chose this guest. It was because of his beard. It reminded her of Captain Grant. The guest also drew a picture of Captain Grant, which ended up looking like the Gorton's Fisherman.)

4/17/12

On our final night had a 1 am visit in the attic above for almost 5 minutes of non-stop movement. When told we were tired and wanted to sleep, said hello to the "spirit" and it stopped. Thanked the "spirit" and went back to sleep. AWESOME!!!

—New Yorkers

11/12/12

We played pool and card games before we started talking to some of the spirits that are still in house. It was really neat to talk to some of them. Great photos of the head stones help us find out who to ask for. We are hoping to meet with Carol to see if we can meet someone new. This was one of the reasons for this stay. Will be sad if we can't talk with Carol. My wife had her pendulum with her and she had a great talk with one of the little black slave girls. She was very excited to speak to her.

—Ghost seekers from the Northeast

(Carol: We do have one young girl whose mother was a slave. The girl is around nine or ten years old and has long, straight black hair. Both she and her mother are buried in the old cemetery behind our property.)

2/19/13

The ghost communication lesson was fun, although we were glad to learn the "Amy" is the least haunted room in the house. I don't know which was creepier, the wind rattling the windows and door on night one or the footsteps in the attic last night.

—Not ghost hunters, just a nice young couple

12/26/13

We had a great time. Last night my husband placed one of the pillows on the bench in front of the bed. When we woke-up the pillow was back on the bed! Creepy!

—New Jersey couple

2/4/14

Had a wonderful night and photographed several orbs and even caught moving orbs on film! No fully formed ghosties or voices to report. It was a unique experience.

—West Brookfield, Massachusetts

5/4/14

Me and my wife came in at 3 AM and as we were opening the door to our room, we suddenly heard footsteps by the stairs on the second floor. We got surprised and scared and could not believe we heard footsteps and nobody was there. Until this we didn't believe in ghosts. The Holy Spirit or something of the like.

—Guests not really looking for a spirit event

9/1/14

Yesterday when we arrived my husband unlocked both doors to the car. When we tried opening the doors to grab our luggage his door was relocked and mine was unlocked. Then when we were watching TV we could hear footsteps above us. The next day my husband could not find a matching sock and before we went to eat he left them at his bedside. We ended up finding the sock on the other side of the room. We definitely were greeted by a few spirits!

—A couple from Connecticut

3/16/15

All I can say is in one word "spooktacula." We will return.

—A great couple

10/24/15

What a beautiful home. We stayed over nite & conducted an investigation. We are from N.Y. & I am part of a paranormal investigation team. This place is warm & inviting. I had an experience, or perhaps it was a dream, I'm not sure but it felt real. While sleeping in bed, I was turned away from my husband & facing the window. I felt someone lay down next to me. The presence was that of a woman. Her head was cradled beneath my chin & she layed beside my chest. I wanted to turn & tell my husband, but I knew if I did she would leave. She was very comforting to me & I fell back asleep. I am looking forward to coming back.

This was the last entry of an experience in the Amy room as of June 2016.

Chapter 19
MARIE ROOM

Three of our rooms do not have little books for guests to write entries about their stays. Some of my guests and I have had experiences in all three of these rooms. The Marie room is in the main building called Captain Grant's. Holly and Margaret are in the Avery home next door. Phenomena have occurred in all of these rooms. The Avery home is where the spirit of the Victim resides and where my husband and I live.

Let's begin with the Marie room, which is on the first floor of Captain Grant's. It is convenient for guests who have difficulty handling staircases. It is also our smallest room. It was once occupied by one of the Taylor sisters, who had so much hatred for each other. It displays a lot of history. The ceiling is open-beamed and the floor is made of nineteenth-century fitted wooden boards. Directly above this room is the Adelaide room. Since the Marie room isn't as haunted as Adelaide is, the hauntings in Adelaide become even more curious. What I mean by that will become evident as you read about the occurrences that I am about to share with you.

In 1998 or thereabout, I had an occasion to sleep in the Marie room. It had just been restored and I was anxious to see how the room felt now that it was done and ready for guests. I had slept in the room many times prior to the completion of the renovation and had never experienced any otherworldly happenings. Around 10:00 p.m. I crawled under the covers and fell asleep, confident in my belief that I was going to have a good night's sleep.

It was almost midnight when I was awakened by a loud noise. I was awake instantly, my eyes wide and peering over the covers. The room was full of the noise of loud, banging furniture moving. I lay there not daring to move. Was the noise outside on the deck or in my room? It sounded like it was everywhere. I slowly pulled the sheet and blanket down from my face and peered over the edge of the comforter. There was no one there. I barely dared to breathe. Maybe it was a raccoon or a squirrel. No, I thought. There was way too much noise for it to be a squirrel. The sides of the walls began to be scratched. I prayed fast and furiously. I didn't dare get out of bed lest I be attacked by some unknown animal or just some unknown thing.

The noise lasted for well over an hour. Then, after more than two more hours of heart-pounding anxiety, I finally fell into a deep sleep. In the morning I awoke and went outside to the deck next to the Marie room. Nothing had been disturbed. Not a thing. This experience, to my knowledge, has never occurred since. I was alone in the house at the time.

A few months later, guests started to report what they had experienced in the Marie room. Many were certain that a spirit had visited them in the night. More than one stated that they had seen an apparition. This room is only one of two bedrooms where an apparition has manifested.

In March of 1997, some guests in the Marie room reported that they had barely slept all night. It appeared to them that the guests in the Adelaide room had come in late and then began to speak loudly and make a lot of noise. They heard someone open the Adelaide door and start walking in the upstairs hallway. This went on for over two hours.

At close to 9:00 the next morning, right before breakfast was to be served, the Marie room guests said they were going to leave. They didn't want to be at breakfast with the Adelaide guests in case words came up between the two parties. One man had gone up to the Adelaide room the night before, knocked on the door, and asked the guests to please be quiet. We decided to give them a free night stay in the future if they wished to come back.

The Marie room in Captain Grant's. Photo credit: Bruce Peter Morin

Finally it was breakfast time and the remaining guests gathered in the dining room. We usually talk with our guests at breakfast, and I decided to ask them how their evening had gone. All but one couple had gone to the casino. The other couple had retired at 10:00 p.m. The casino-goers were all in bed by 11:00 p.m. "Did anyone hear someone come in?" I asked. They all said no. "How was everyone's night? Did all of you sleep well?" One guest said that it was really quiet.

At this point I told the guests what had happened to the guests in the Marie room. They were all dumbfounded. We knew the noise was not caused by anyone looking for a room. We asked the guests in the Adelaide room if they had heard someone knock on their door. They denied hearing anything. We knew that no one had driven up the driveway and gone in the house. Our security system alerts us to that. We all wondered who the Marie room guests had heard.

Perhaps the strangest thing that has ever happened in the Marie room actually occurred in the Adelaide room. This was prior to the little leather-bound books being placed in the upper rooms. The couple in the Adelaide room were regular guests of ours, having visited several times. On one particular night, their door opened and then closed by itself. No big deal, they told me. But then the TV went off and they had to turn it on again. The infamous shower curtain hurled itself onto the floor and lay there until morning. The guests weren't about to get out of bed and hang it up again.

The home at this time was heated by steam. This is one of the best types of heat that a home can have. As the boiler heats up, steam rises through pipes running from the basement to the first floor and then to the second floor. The pipes for the Adelaide room run through the Marie room. If it gets too warm in a room, the guests can turn down a shut-off valve but the pipe running to the next floor continues to offer heat. The guests in the Marie room had done that very thing—turned down their valve when the room was comfortable. Following this, they went to bed.

In the Adelaide room above them, the heat kept cranking out until the room was over 80 degrees. The guests in the Adelaide room said, the next morning, that no matter what they did, the heat just kept pouring out of the radiator. Eventually they opened a window to help the room cool off. This occurred in the heart of winter. At breakfast we asked the couple in the Marie room if their room was too warm. It wasn't. Also the steam pipe leading to the Adelaide room was cold when they touched it but the steam radiator in the Adelaide room was hot, an impossibility. The Adelaide couple was moved to the Margaret room and spent the next night restfully. This has never happened since and the couple has never returned.

All in all, the Marie room is spiritually quiet. It is still heated by steam, but the Adelaide room is now heated by a gas fireplace. For us it means that event will never happen again.

There is one event that happened that had us chuckling a bit one morning. We had guests staying in the Adelaide room. They were the only guests we had that night. We live in the Avery house next door and walk over to the Grant house each morning to serve breakfast. That morning was no exception, but on the way over we noticed that one of the cars was missing from the parking lot. As we entered the kitchen we saw a note on the island. The guests had left in the middle of the night. They had heard a man talking, a woman singing, people laughing, etc. The guests wrote that they were too scared to stay and left for home. Our TVs at that time could be programmed to act as alarm clocks, going on at a designated time. I decided to check out the Marie room, and sure enough the TV was on.

We felt bad that our guests had experienced such fear, but we also shook our heads at how much fear we can create in our own minds.

In the Amy room, the identical thing happened. We had a wedding at the inn. The bride and groom slept in the Amy room and immediate family members filled the rest of the rooms. At 2:00 a.m. the Amy room TV blasted on. It was an old George Raft gangster movie. At breakfast the next morning, the family said they all woke up to a man yelling, "I'm going to kill you!" They all thought that the newlyweds had had a terrible argument. I am glad to say that we no longer have those TVs.

Chapter 20
THE AVERY HOME

The Avery home was built in 1790 and is also listed on the National Register of Historic Places. It is thirty-six years newer than the Captain Grant house. We don't know if this dating is entirely accurate. It has been rumored that the home actually dates from the 1600s and was originally where a man named Samuel had his blacksmith shop. A blacksmith did not have the income of a sea captain, and this home reflects that reality. Whereas Captain Grant's home has ceilings seven feet six inches high, the Avery home has ceilings that are six feet six inches high. The rooms are also smaller, and when I purchased the home each room had a heavy door shutting it off from the other rooms. This meant that each room could maintain its heat with its fireplace. It also meant less draw of cold air going up the chimney.

The addition to the Avery home was added to the back in 1827. Tadashi and I live on the second and third floors of this home. In 1999 we opened up for rent the two downstairs bedrooms, the Margaret room and the Holly room. These rooms both face the new cemetery across the street. The entry to the cemetery is directly in front of the Margaret room window.

Margaret Room

Looking out of one of the two front windows of the Margaret room you see the road leading into the current Poquetanuck Cemetery. The stone pillars of the cemetery date it to 1903, but the headstones go back as far as the 1700s.

The Margaret room in the Avery home. Photo credit: Bruce Peter Morin

I believe the strangest ghost event that has occurred in the Margaret room happened to a couple who had no interest in the paranormal. They had come to stay with us while on vacation. They had planned to visit Mystic and the two casinos. Both were lawyers. That weekend all of our rooms were full, giving us fourteen guests for breakfast. All of the other guests were staying with us in hopes of having something unearthly happen to them. None of them experienced anything unusual. At breakfast they were laughing and having a good time making fun of each other about wanting to see a ghost. This good time lasted for almost an hour while the guests in the Margaret room sat at the table remaining quiet. Finally one of the guests noticed their silence, looked at them, and said, "You are both so quiet. Are you here for the ghosts?"

They answered with a strong NO. Everyone was abruptly silent. Then the woman from the Margaret room said, "I think all of you would have liked to stay in our room last night."

"Did something happen?" another woman asked.

That is when the conversation changed dramatically and went something like this, with the wife doing most of the speaking. All others at the table sat and stared in disbelief.

"We both woke up around 2:00 a.m.," said the woman. "Standing at the bottom of the bed were four people, or I guess spirits. There was a man, woman, boy, and girl. They were all dressed differently. They looked like they had come from a different period of time."

"What did they do?" asked another woman.

"Nothing. They just stood there and looked at us. I was frightened, but nothing happened. I was really shook up, and John just held me until I stopped shaking. Then they faded away as if they had never been there."

The others were stunned. I remember someone saying, "I wish we had been there. I think."

I didn't tell the guests what had happened to me that night. My husband and I have our bedroom directly above the Margaret room. At 2:00 a.m. I had a terrible nightmare. I dreamed that spirits had come out of the cemetery across the road and had entered the Margaret room through the front wall of the house. My dream went on and I saw the spirits attempting to come up through the ceiling and up the stairs to where I was sleeping. In my dream I thought they were coming for me. I screamed and my husband woke me up. This is what he said.

"You're having a nightmare. You must be quiet. There is something going on in the Margaret room downstairs and I don't want to disturb our guests. We can't hear what people are saying, but if they are loud enough we can hear muffled voices." He went on. "Someone is sobbing and sounds scared. What happened to you?"

I spoke quietly and told him my dream. He held me for a long time and I finally fell asleep. After listening to the guest, I believe that my dream may have had some truth to it.

This happened around the summer of 2010 and thank God never again. It is the room where my sister-in-law Margaret, whom the room is named after, sleeps when she comes to visit. She repeatedly tells us how much she likes the room.

Holly Room

The Holly room is directly across the hall from the Margaret room. The two rooms look entirely different. Margaret has a bit of a Victorian flair, whereas Holly looks eighteenth century. The Holly ceiling is covered with its original beams. They are nearly as hard as iron. The room has a fireplace that Tadashi fashioned after an original eighteenth-century fireplace that I saw in a *Country Home* magazine. Above this fireplace is a painting that is a copy of a small section of the ceiling in the Sistine Chapel.

Before I purchased Captain Grant's, the Holly room was where I spent most of my hours at home. It had no fireplace then, just an old cast-iron stove that we burned wood logs in to warm up the room in winter. The stove was oddly placed in the middle of the room. In the 1700s this room would have been called a keeping room. It was where you kept your guests warm when they came to call. In the cellar directly below the room is a wall that I believe was the foundation for the original kitchen. The kitchen was moved to the back of the house when the new addition was added. It has a massive foundation.

The Holly room in the Avery house. Photo credit: Bruce Peter Morin

The office for Captain Grant's is directly above the Holly room. On occasion we hear things going on in the room. The most profound event was a loud crash followed by a piece of furniture being moved. It was early evening and both my husband and I were standing at the top of the stairs when the incident occurred. The stairs lead down to the open door of the Holly room. We asked, "Who is there?" No one answered. We slowly walked down the steps. Then we looked everywhere. Nothing had been disturbed, not one little thing, and both doors to the outside were locked. We were dumbfounded. We both shook our heads and headed back upstairs.

We typically spend three to four hours a day in the office. Frequently we hear voices. In February of 2016 we distinctly heard two people speaking. They were having a conversation right below us in the Holly room. I turned to my husband, who was behind me at his desk, and asked him if he could hear people talking. He said, "Yes. There must be somebody down there." He was thinking it must be a staff member or a guest.

I said, "Who would it be? We have no guests, and the staff went home an hour ago."

He said, "You're right. I will go down and see who's there."

Well, no one was there and when he went into the Holly room the talking stopped. He came back up to the office and the Holly conversation started up again. We just let them talk and continued to work on our computers.

The sounds in this room vary. When I wake up at night or in the early morning I frequently can hear a man talking. He sounds like a radio talk show host. His speech has a steady rhythm to it. It sometimes continues for almost an hour. It may continue longer, but I end up falling asleep and can't attest to anything longer than an hour.

We also hear singing. It sounds like a female voice. This doesn't occur as often but is the most unusual sound to listen to. There is never a specific tune or song. It is simply a lilt of sounds. It reminds us of someone who is happy and enjoying the day.

Moving Forward

I have taken you, the reader, through a representative recollection of our guests and my experiences with the spirits at Captain Grant's and the Avery home. There is more ground to cover, however, and we will get to that soon, but first I'd like to summarize my thoughts to date.

It is pretty clear that we have a number of spirits in residence, and there has been ample proof of that. While we do not advertise it, our B&B qualifies as being "haunted" and certainly has that reputation on the internet.

That I can talk to these spirits may require a little faith on your part, but I and any number of guests are convinced that there is proof of that. Hopefully, having read this far, you are convinced also. The spirits represent or were people who once existed but now are dead. The people lived in different times, but their spirits are simultaneously here. For lack of a better term, I refer to the spirits as the "souls" of these people. Soul is a powerful word to attach to these spirits, but it does seem to fit our understanding of the word. In later chapters, we will find further justification for believing these spirits are, in fact, souls.

I have long accepted the spirits at Captain Grant's and am grateful for my ability to hold "conversations" with them, even though I am not always sure I am getting truthful responses. Over time, as I have gotten to "know" the spirits better, I have gotten better at sorting out what is likely to be true and what is not.

With my evolving comfort level with the resident spirits, I decided I wanted to know more about the spirit world in the hope that I could learn about the various aspects of the afterlife and share that information with others. So I decided to continue these conversations, focusing on what was happening in the spirit world, "life" in the spirit world, and some controversial subjects such as reincarnation, heaven, and hell.

My Roman Catholic upbringing continues to enter my thoughts. It is the intertwining thread that runs through all of what I write. I continue to explore the afterlife but at times with a distinct struggle.

I wonder if I should just let it all remain a mystery. Then curiosity takes over and I begin to explore again.

Much of what I write is controversial. I ask that you read with an open mind and know that what is written is what I have honestly heard and observed. It doesn't mean that it is correct. So far nothing concrete has been proven by anyone. This story is just another view.

Chapter 21
THE GATHERING

In September of 2015, events in the spirit world began to change. The spirits were beginning to gather. I also had one of those memorable decade birthdays. My husband and sister decided to throw me a party, with cousins coming from three states. This is only important to the extent that they started asking me questions about the spirits. "Are they still here?" Yes. "Are there still twelve of them in the house?" Yes. "Do you communicate with them on a regular basis?" "No." In fact, I hadn't had a conversation with the spirits for at least a couple of months. I had decided that I should speak more to the living than to the dead. Anyway, it was high season at the B&B and there really wasn't much time.

After thinking about the questions I was asked, I decided to take my rods and speak with the spirits in private. My family stayed for two weeks, and it was hard to find time to be by myself. One morning, prior to getting breakfast started, I went up to the game room, took out my rods, and had what turned out to be one very eye-opening conversation.

I started by asking who I was speaking to. It turned out to be Daniel.

"Daniel, are there still twelve of you in the house?"

"Yes." When he answered, the rods moved around a bit. I wondered why and decided to probe further.

"Daniel, are there more than twelve of you in the house?"

"Yes." This was a clear answer, with the rods moving straight out sideways in short order.

"Okay. Are there more than twenty spirits in the house?" Again the rods opened wide, indicating an answer of yes.

It was just then that relatives began to enter the kitchen. I thanked Daniel, ran down to help prepare breakfast, and quickly put my rods away. My mind was trying to focus on breakfast, but I couldn't help thinking about the additional spirits. I knew that I didn't have an actual count. According to Daniel, there were now at least twenty spirits in the house. Perhaps there were even more.

I decided to try speaking with the spirits again as soon as my relatives left. It didn't happen. October is our third busiest month, falling just behind July and August. I was left waiting for November, but November was unusually good for the business that year.

I gave a ghost communication lesson in November but focused on my guests and not the questions still burning in my mind. Nonetheless, it was an interesting session that went something like this.

The woman who was part of the lesson was an engineer from Europe who asked a lot of scientific questions. My husband is also an engineer, so I asked him to join us in the game room. The man had brought a gaussmeter to detect electromagnetic fields. The woman asked questions such as "Who says that the red line on that meter means there is a ghost present? Who made that decision and under what circumstances?" My husband, Tadashi, was an electrical engineer. The woman was a civil engineer. Tadashi then explained what was happening and decided to try and demonstrate an electrical proof. Above the poker table where we were sitting was a chandelier. Tadashi stated that if the gaussmeter was sensitive, it should register electromagnetic fields when it was held up to the light. It did not register. It didn't matter if the light was turned off or on.

The immediate conclusion to this experiment was that the meter was faulty. So I took the rods that the guests used and touched them to the meter. Nothing happened. I had my personal rods that had been given to me. I took them in my hands and touched the meter, which registered as far into the red as it could go. All of us sat and stared at the meter and then at my rods. Then everyone looked at me. Next I laid the rods on the meter without touching them. It registered back to nothing. Then I touched the meter with my hand, and still nothing. It took the combination of my holding the rods for the meter to register. The rods or my own touch could not make the meter read in the red. We left the room not being able to figure out what had just happened. No explanation came to mind.

It was in November that the spirits began to manifest more than they ever had before. One guest captured dozens of orbs in the meadow between the old cemetery and the house. "Well," I thought, "this could be dust particles, but maybe not." The guest also captured at least fifty orbs on our outdoor deck. I was fascinated and thought, "What is happening?"

Then a father with his two sons came and stayed in the Elizabeth room. When they came down the following morning for breakfast, they had quite a story to tell. The day before they had decided to go out to the old cemetery behind the house. The youngest son had left his iPad on the dresser, upside down and turned off. They locked the door and went for their walk. At Captain Grant's the doors automatically lock, but they might not have been aware of that fact.

When they got back from their trek across the meadow, they had quite a surprise waiting for them. The door to their room was open. The upside-down iPad was now right-side up. On its face was an image of a man standing in their doorway. The man was large and black. His shoulders reached from one side of the door to the other. His head reached to the top of the door opening. We could tell that the man was entirely bald, but that was all. No features could be seen. I asked for a copy of what they had, but never received one. The boy's iPad was locked up. He couldn't shut it down or do anything with it.

Soon after, a week or two at most, another couple came and stayed in the Elizabeth room. They decided to take a picture of their naked feet lying at the end of the bed. Dozens of orbs appeared. They immediately saw orbs everywhere through their iPhone and decided to film the event. The orbs were flying in all directions. One large streak of light flew from behind their heads down above the comforter and then up and over the fireplace. Just to let my readers know, the fireplace is sealed, so no ash or cinders are possible in the room. (Ash and cinders could also produce orbs.) I have seen hundreds of orb pictures, but this was the most astonishing of all. The couple were kind enough to download the photo for me on my husband's computer.

It was the first week of December and business was slow. Now I had time to talk to Daniel. I walked over to the B&B and sat down in the kitchen at our high table. My rods were in my hands. My heart was pounding. I knew something was happening but didn't know what.

"Daniel, are you here?"

"Yes."

"Would you tell me how many spirits are now in the house?"

"Yes."

"Are there more than twenty?"

"Yes."

"Thirty?"

"Yes."

And so on until I got to sixty, for which I got a no response.

I then went through each number over fifty. I now had fifty-six spirits in the house. It was the beginning of December 2015.

"Daniel, are the spirits gathering?"

"Yes."

"Is this world affecting your world?"

"Yes."

"Are spirits gathering in other places around the world?"

"Yes."

"All over the world?"

"Yes."

"Is something going to happen between our worlds?"

"Yes."

I needed to sleep on this. I had to gather my thoughts. I needed to speak with several spirits, not just Daniel.

"Does anyone else know about this?" I asked myself. "Or am I the only one?" I prayed not. "God, what is going on?" For the first time I began to feel apprehensive. "I am an ordinary person who knows extraordinary things. Why?" And I started to doubt what I was learning.

My head spun for a while, but I had a business to run so I had to attend to my duties. I had a reservation due in my register, and on December 28 they arrived for a four-day stay. The wife was a reverend and also a well-known psychic. We talked. She knew about the gathering or amassing of the spirits, as she called it. "The time is coming" was her comment when we spoke.

What she spoke about was good versus evil. She told me that good will enter into this world through the gathering of spirits. Evil individuals will be approached and they will have to decide which side they are going to take: good or evil. If they choose evil they will die. I was never told how this death will occur.

After my conversations with her, I had thoughts for communicating with the spirits—questions that I could ask.

It was January of 2016. I decided that I had to speak with the spirits. I headed over to the B&B but forgot my rods at home. It was cold outside and I decided that I would use the rods that I had bought for our guests to use. I don't normally use those rods. They're a bit heavy for me and I find that I get tired much sooner. I have to give off my energy to communicate with the spirits, so the weight of the rods is critical.

John, our right-hand man, was repairing the dining room floor at the time, so I decided to go up to the game room, where I would have optimum privacy.

I sat at the poker table, took the rods out of their pouch, and found them surprisingly comfortable. I started in my usual manner, finding out who I was talking with and asking if they knew anything about the subject that I was about to question them on. I reached Deborah Adams. I knew in an instant it was her. The rods hugged my cheeks and swung back and forth several times. The following is our conversation.

"Deborah, are there still fifty-six souls in the house?"

"No." The rods crossed.

"Are there fewer souls in the house now?"

"No."

"Are there more souls in the house?"

"Yes."

I did the usual counting, going up to 55, then 60, and lastly 65. After doing the 61, 62, 63 exploration, I had the exact count. There were now 63 spirits at Captain Grant's. I led out a big sigh and went on.

"Are the souls going to be involved in an event on Earth?"
"Yes."
"Are the angels going to be involved in this event?"
"No."

I was surprised by this and decided to ask about God.

"Is God going to be involved?"
"Yes."
"Are people going to be judged by God?"
"Yes."
"Is this the final judgment?"
"No."
"Are both the good and the bad going to be judged?"
"Yes."
"Will the bad people die?"
"No."
"Will they remain on Earth?"
"Yes."
"Will the good people die?"

With this question the rods went back and forth. I had a feeling that Deborah didn't know how to answer the question. She finally answered no.

"Are the good people going to go somewhere off of this Earth?"
"Yes."

Okay, now where do they go? I wondered.

"Do they go to the spirit world?" I asked. "The one where you are?"

"No."

"Do they go to heaven?"

"No."

"Do they remain on Earth with the evil people?"

"No."

Now I was frustrated. Just what happens to the good people? I thought of purgatory or a holding cell in a jail. So I decided to try that route. After a couple more minutes of thinking over different scenarios, I decided on the holding cell approach.

"Deborah, is God going to have all of the good people stay someplace safe that he has made for them?"

"Yes."

"Is this the great judgment that is talked about in the Bible and throughout the Christian world?"

"No."

I searched my mind for more questions. Finally, I had one.

"Is this the Rapture that some Christians talk about?"

"Yes."

I put the rods down due to phone calls. After I was finished with phone business, I hung up and made the decision to talk to another spirit. I thought that Mercy was the best choice to answer my inquiries.

"Mercy, will you talk to me? Are you here?"

The rods immediately responded by opening wide.

"Thank you, Mercy. Have you been listening to Deborah?"

"Yes."

"Is everything she said correct?"

"No."

I decided to take a stab in the dark. "Is this about hell and where evil people go?"

"Yes."

"All of the spirits have told me that there is no hell. Could it be that there is no hell as we understand it to be?"

"Yes."

"Could it be a very dark place devoid of light and goodness? A place where there is no God?" My friend Abby and her experience with being touched by Father D'Orio had come to mind. Had she experienced hell or a type of hell? I write about Abby's and my experience in the next chapter.

"Yes."

"Spirits are gathering here and around the world. Is this true?"

"Yes."

"Are evil spirits also gathering around the world?"

"Yes."

"Is there going to be a war?"

"Yes."

"Is this war going to take place between evil and good? Are the spirits going to be part of this war?"

"Yes."

"Is this war going to last for seven years?" I guessed seven years because that is what the Bible prophesy states.

"Yes."

"Do you know when it will start?"

"No."

"I want to ask some question about religion. Will you answer them for me?"

"Yes."

"Did God ever break his covenant with the Jewish people?"

"No."

"Does he have a new covenant with Christian people?"

"Yes."

I ran down a list of world religions and then came to a surprising bit of information. It had to do with the American Indians from the Great Plains states. This is how the conversation went.

"Mercy, does God have a covenant with the American Indians?"
"Yes."
"Did God give them the White Buffalo Woman?"
"Yes."
"Well, it seems that God appears to many people in many ways," I said to myself.

I thought a lot about the material in this chapter. If what the spirits tell me is true, I believe that we are headed toward what has been prophesied for millennia: the end of life on this planet as we know it. If this is the case, I certainly hope that it becomes a kinder and better world.

I spent a fair amount of time wondering if I should delete this chapter, but after much contemplation I decided to keep it in the book. It is what it is. I thought about my last reincarnation and decided that maybe I mocked God or denied my faith and that is why I am here now—to right that wrong. That made my final decision for me.

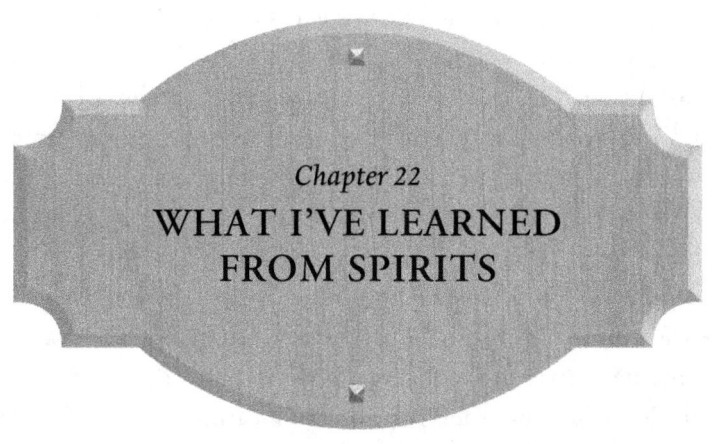

Chapter 22
WHAT I'VE LEARNED FROM SPIRITS

Reincarnation

I started to explore reincarnation during my second year of using the L-rods. At a session with eight guests I decided that I would ask the spirit if someone at the table had lived another life. The rods opened, so I asked the spirit to point to that individual. The spirit did. From that time on, it is one of the common questions that I ask during a session.

I have used the L-rods throughout the United States. I have had hundreds of spirit conversations. All of the spirits that I communicate with give me the same answers about being reborn.

None of them ever want to be reborn, except for Pete. They much prefer the realm that they are in over the world we live in.

Most of these spirits with past lives have lived about four or five lives. Will that be a larger number as the human race remains on Earth? Perhaps. Of course there are spirits that are on their second life and those that have had many more. The most lives that I have encountered in one spirit is seven. One book on past lives that I've read, called *Many Lives, Many Masters*, focuses on a woman who has had eighty-six lives. So no one answer is correct. My findings are simply my findings and nothing more.

Reincarnation doesn't seem to happen immediately after death. I know of only one that happened within the same century in which the person lived and died. According to my spirits, most spirits don't come back until somewhere between two and three hundred years later. Pete lived in the 1600s and still has not been reincarnated. I also have never had a spirit tell me that their first life was before the time of Christ. I am curious about this and hope to find the answer in the future. I believe that it is probably just a coincidence and that souls have been reincarnating since they first entered a human being.

When I asked the spirits if they have a choice in who they will be when they are reborn, they all said no. That is a lot of nos. They also don't have a choice in when they come back or if they are male or female. God makes all the decisions. That is God the almighty father, not his son. When they are reborn, there is no warning. One second they are in the spirit world and the next they are in a newborn body.

When asked if the soul enters the body at the time of fertilization, the answer from the spirits was again a no. The soul enters the baby at the exact time of birth, and it leaves at the exact time of death.

The spirits that have lived multiple lives all agree that they need to right a wrong that occurred in a past life. This wrong was committed by them. When that wrong is righted, they will cease to be reincarnated and then can seek out the light.

When we are born, only our soul remembers. We don't. It is rare for an individual to remember a past life, and yet I have heard of a few that do. This, of course, presents a dilemma. How are we supposed to know what we have to correct about our lives? Using Pete as an example, he has lived four lives and has murdered someone in three of those lives. Quite frankly, I am a little worried about Pete being reborn again. God must have knowledge that Pete will eventually make the right decisions, and Christianity as a whole says that God has given us free will while we are alive on Earth. It seems more and more that there are no definitive answers, only more questions.

I wonder about myself. I was raised Roman Catholic. I became engrossed in the Bible in my forties and read everything I could get my hands on concerning Bible prophesy, Jesus Christ, the Apostles, and on and on. I have probably read the book of Revelation ten times and the book of Daniel another six times. The book of Revelation began to make sense to me when I looked at it as letters to the ages instead of letters to churches. The last letter, Laodicea, would be the lifetime that we are in now. Then it all made sense to me. This was wonderful, as I grew more aware of what was happening in my world.

Then I discovered the L-rods and everything became a confusion. Now I know that I am on my fourth life and the spirit Mercy is waiting for my husband to die so they can go to heaven together. At times I feel a little crazy. Well, I love my husband and she can't have him. Besides, when he dies his spirit will be the spirit of my husband and not Captain Grant.

This brings up another aspect of reincarnation that I have yet to understand. When a person dies, it seems as if the spirit remains that person until the spirit is reborn. If that is the case, then my husband will not know Mercy, and she is waiting futilely.

I have asked the spirits if I am doing the right thing this time around. They assure me that this reincarnation is the last and say that I will have a chance at heaven. Of course this is future knowledge and do they really know? Once I took a break from thinking about reincarnation and decided to read a book on it instead. This is the book that I mentioned previously, *Many Lives, Many Masters*, written by a well-known psychiatrist named Brian L. Weiss, MD. It centers on a patient whom he treated with past-life regression therapy. This patient had lived eighty-six times. When she died in one life, she ascended and then was quickly put into another life. She also lived before the time of Christ. This is why I now look at what I learned earlier from the people I interviewed as just a coincidence in the sense that none of them had ever lived prior to the time of Christ. I decided to ask a spirit about this. I spoke with Mercy's daughter.

"I read a book on reincarnation and the writer talked about someone dying and then being immediately sent into another newborn person. Is this true?"

She answered with a NO.

So then I asked, "Can someone be reincarnated in a very short time? Let's say in one day's time in our world."

The rods said yes.

So I think that in my terminology I would say that they die, ascend, experience their death by looking at their body, and then are reborn. I also asked her if this was common and she answered with another yes.

The spirits that I interview, that psychics listen to, and that others see have been here for some time. If they didn't, then none of us would have contact with the spirit world. They wouldn't exist in the spirit world long enough for us to make contact.

Time

In all of my communication with the spirit world, I have heard one constant: they cannot predict the future. "Only God knows the future" is what every one of them has said to me. After writing the previous chapter, "The Gathering," I decided that I wanted to know how the spirits experience time. I have been told by several mediums and psychics that they do not experience time. Not like we do, in any case.

"Daniel, will you speak to me?" The rods swung wildly and I got a hug. "Hi, Deborah," I said. I hated to tell her that I needed to talk with Daniel. It had been a long time since we had had a chat. The rods again gave me a hug and I knew that she was letting go and handing me over to Daniel.

"Daniel, are you here?" I asked again.

The rods opened wide and then I got a hug with one rod.

"Thank you, Daniel," I said. "I would like to talk to you about time."

The rods opened up, communicating an approval of the conversation.

"Do you experience time in the same way that we who are alive experience time?"

The rods crossed, giving a no answer.

"Can you experience future time?"

I expected to get a no answer, and that is just what happened.

"It appears that reincarnation takes about two hundred to three hundred years. Do you experience it in that time frame?"

"No." It was a clear no, but there was also some movement of the rods back and forth.

"Do you experience time at all?"

The rods moved slowly, with hesitation. Then Daniel said no.

Then I thought to myself, while speaking out loud, "Is there something that I'm not asking?"

"Yes," Daniel answered, somewhat startling me since I had been deep in thought.

"Is this beyond my understanding?"

Now the rods wavered back and forth.

"Do you not know the answer to this question?"

Daniel responded with a definite no.

"Okay, where do I go from here?" I wondered. I had started to think about time most recently with the gathering of the spirits. Questions kept popping up in my head about the war that was coming. When? How soon? The spirits don't know, only God knows. The spirits have said it will be soon. Well, what does "soon" mean to them? I was back at the beginning with my time questions.

I knew that I needed a time reference that would work for both Daniel and me. What if my lifetime was the reference? Would that work? I decided to find out.

"Daniel, I want to ask you another question about the gathering of spirits and the spirit war. Do you believe it will happen in my lifetime?"

Daniel immediately answered with a yes.

I was a bit dubious since he had also told me he couldn't predict the future. My mind was spinning. What should I ask next? What Daniel had just told me meant that he believes he will shortly be coming back to the world where I live. I wondered how he felt about that. All of the spirits, with the exception of Pete, don't want to come back to this world. Now they're going to fight a war. What will happen to them after the war? There was this spirit world dilemma. Will they come back to our world or go back to waiting to be reincarnated again? I remembered that one of the spirits said that if they hadn't corrected the wrong they had committed or finished their quest, they would have come back to Earth as someone else. How did they feel about this? I decided to push on with Daniel, but I also wanted to speak with another spirit to get a second opinion.

First I wanted to find out what will happen to the spirits after the war. So I asked Daniel, "Will you come back to Earth as a living human being after the war?"

He answered yes.

"Will you be coming back as Daniel?"

"No."

I wondered how he felt about that, but he couldn't answer that type of question for me.

"Does this matter to you?"

"No," he answered, without hesitation.

"Daniel, thank you. I would like to speak with Mercy if she is here."

"Yes." The rods opened wide and I asked Mercy if she was willing to talk with me.

"Yes," she answered and then gave me a hug.

"Have you been listening to Daniel and I converse?"

The rods indicated a yes.

"Do you agree with what he said to me?"

Another yes.

At this point I wanted to take a break and head for my office. I informed both Daniel and Mercy that I was leaving but would be back to talk with them soon.

I got a cup of coffee and then headed across the yard. I sat down at the computer and began to write down everything I had been told while it was still fresh in my memory.

Two days later, I grabbed my personal rods and headed for the game room again. I couldn't think. I was at a crossroads. Finally I held the rods and asked to speak to Mercy, but even though she was there I got a new spirit to talk with me.

We chatted back and forth for a few minutes. I decided not to talk to her about time, but I still wanted to acknowledge her presence and find out who she was.

"Did you ever live in this house?"

"Yes."

"Would you please point to where your body is buried?"

I was sitting with my back facing the newer cemetery from the 1800s. Slowly the rods turned and were pointing directly across the street. She had to have died later than the other spirits that I had talked to.

"Did you die in the 1900s?"

The rods turned slowly, confirming a yes answer. She moved the rods slower than the spirits I usually talk with, which was indicative of a spirit that has not conversed with a live person before.

I wanted to find out her age at death and asked if she was older than sixty.

"No."

Going down ten years at a time, I finally got to twenty. "Were you older than twenty?"

"Yes."

It turns out that she died at age twenty-one of an illness.

"Were you ever married?"

"Yes."

"Did you have children?"

"Yes."

"More than one?"

"Yes." With this answer the rods moved back and forth, as if she wasn't certain of her answer.

"Did you lose a child in childbirth?"

"Yes."

I had deviated from my questions on time and wanted to return to my inquiries on that subject. I thanked the new spirit for talking to me and put my rods down on the table.

I think about what I've learned from the spirits about the subject of time. Spirits don't experience time the same way that we do. They may not experience time at all. They can't experience future time, only present time. Still, Daniel had indicated that there was a question about time that I was not asking. He couldn't answer the question of whether or not I would be able to understand time in the spirit world while I am still alive. Where is Stephen Hawking when you need him?

I searched my library for the book that I have on time by Hawking but couldn't find it anywhere. I had an idea pop up in my head and had to check it out immediately. I grabbed my rods on the run and headed next door to the kitchen. No one was there. The kitchen was comfortably warm and cozy. It was late afternoon by then and the sun was hanging low in the sky. I left the lights off, giving the kitchen just the right feel for my new investigation into time.

I held out the rods and asked for Mercy.

"Mercy, are you here?"

"Yes."

"I have questions about dimensional worlds. Do you think you might be able to answer some questions on that subject?"

The rods quivered, then she answered yes.

"I'm going to retrace some questions that I have already asked Daniel. Please bear with me on this. Do the spirits live in a two-dimensional world?"

"No."

I suspected that answer. It was the same one that Daniel had given me. "Do you live in a one-dimensional world?"

"Yes."

At that point I wondered if the spirits even understand what dimensional world they live in.

Then I asked, "If you live in a one-dimensional world, that world is a straight line that can go in only one direction. There would be no up or down or sideways. Is that what your world is like?"

"No."

This answer was incorrect, since that is exactly what a one-dimensional world is. Then I thought about what they could be trying to tell me.

"Okay," I said to myself. "Here goes." I took a deep breath and asked, "Is your one-dimensional world time?"

"Yes."

Oh my God. I was stunned and shaking. "Is this the question that Daniel wanted me to ask?"

"Yes," she said, with no hesitation.

"Is heaven also in time?"

"Yes."

My thoughts went to what I have read about time. It is sometimes referred to as the fourth dimension. I would like to think that God and the spirits live in more dimensions than we do, not fewer.

Also, as far as I know, time is a constant. It always was and always will be. The one thing that is not constant is that time is not the same throughout the universe. What is a year on Earth may be two months on a distant asteroid. This is also a theory. Could the spirits live in one part of time and heaven be in another part of time? I decided to ask.

"Mercy, could the spirits live in one part of time, with heaven being in another part of time?"

"Yes."

I remembered my Catholic upbringing. The nuns told us that God always was and always would be. If what Mercy had told me about time was true, then the Sisters' statements could also be true. It was mind-boggling. I just couldn't quite believe what I had just discovered. This is why souls are eternal. All in all, there was too much to digest. Was I really getting any truths about anything from the spirits?

I decided to take a break from writing and communicating with the spirits. I had to let my brain rest and absorb what I had been told. It was then that I read two very different books, one on reincarnation and one on time.

In the book *About Time* by Paul Davies, time is considered a fourth dimension. If the spirits live in the fourth dimension, then they should be able to materialize and show width and height. This, of course, they have done on many occasions. It appeared that what the spirits were trying to tell me is not correct on a scientific level. I decided to leave these questions behind and move on.

The War

Prophecies about the "end times" have been made for centuries. Three of the most famous sources are the Bible, Nostradamus, and a self-proclaimed prophet of the twentieth century named William Marrion Branham. Tim LaHaye and Jerry B. Jenkins authored the Left Behind series of twelve books about the last seven years prior to Christ's return. Believers have spoken of the Rapture, where people are taken off the Earth and then seven years of strife commence until the Great War occurs.

All of the prophesies are similar. The focus of nearly every one is the struggle between good and evil. The main problem is that different people believe different things about what is good and what is evil. I believe it is the nature of humankind to want to end evil in the world. Since we don't seem to be doing very well at that task, some of us, at least, are hoping that the world of spirits can help or maybe even solve the problem.

Over Valentine's weekend that year, the bed and breakfast was full of guests. The only place to have privacy to speak with the spirits about this subject was in my office in the Avery house. When I had tried that before, I had gotten a spirit playing games with me and pretending to be Mercy. Still, I had been told by two spirits that another two spirits are always with me. Maybe they would talk to me. I made the decision to attempt communication with them at my desk.

I spoke with the woman who was the Victim. She did not know about the gathering of good spirits but she did know about the gathering of evil spirits. I found this interesting. I had done an exorcism in the 1980s in the Avery home and was still skeptical about the current spirits in that house. I decided that I was going to end the session and wait until I went back to the game room in the other house. I am very protective of myself when it comes to the dark side of the spirit world. I asked myself, "Why does she know of the bad spirits gathering and not the good?" I don't think I wanted to know. After all, Tadashi and I live in that home.

There are those two words staring at me: Good. Bad. Just what makes a person either one in the spirit world? In our three-dimensional world we have an idea of what those two words mean. There are different codes for different religions and separate norms and customs for all of the earth's people. For instance, at one time it was acceptable for men in the Mormon religion to have multiple wives. As time continued this practice became frowned upon and is rare today. In the centuries prior to Christ, Israeli men had concubines. Today it in not rare for a woman to bear a child for a couple who can't bear one for themselves. How we think of morality and sin is constantly changing. I believe that the spirits have to live by God's law, but we don't know for certain just what that law is. Most Christians and Jews would think of it as the Ten Commandments.

When this war begins, it will be up to each one of us to sort that question out.

In thinking about this war, I wonder how it will be fought. Will it be in the usual way, with weapons and armies, or will there be an alternative method at work?

I again gripped my rods and headed to our outdoor deck. The sun was shining and the warm spring air brought joy after the long winter.

I talked to Mercy about this war. She indicated that it would be fought by the spirit world. They would be fighting for the souls of us on Earth. I thought that was already going on, but she said that this was going to be different. I asked her if countries such as China, the United States, Great Britain, Russia, and all the others would still exist after this war, and she said no. There would be one central government for the entire globe and it would be centered in Southern Europe. I thought to myself, "I guess I will have to wait and see. Only time will tell."

Heaven

Each and every spirit that I have communicated with confirms that there is a heaven. They just don't know what it is like. I had a guest that tried to send Deborah Adams to heaven. Instead, Deborah hid in her grave and didn't come back to the house for about two months. When I tried to convince Adelaide to go to the light, she stopped talking to me. She did start communicating with me again later that month. Clearly not everyone has an urgent desire to go there.

I visited heaven once. I was in my thirties and had a seriously ill daughter. This preoccupied my thoughts as I looked everywhere for a cure. I was living in Minnesota not far from my favorite aunt, Shirley. She told me about a Father D'Orio who had the power to heal and asked me to go to a mass with her where he was the presiding priest. My aunt was very convincing. So, with high hopes for a miracle, my daughter and I made the trip to St. Cloud, Minnesota, where Father D'Orio was going to hold Mass. I did not know what to expect but was never deterred by new experiences.

The Catholic Mass started. I don't remember a lot of what happened, just the electricity in the air. I could feel it all around me. I was fully glued to the altar. Then my daughter became hot. Not a bad hot, just an intense warm. I thought, "God is with her." Then my knees became hot and the warmth traveled down to my feet. My toes were hot. I just stood there looking down at them. I had a condition in the middle toe on each of my feet that was the result of a skating incident when I was a young child. At times my toes would feel like they were broken and I could barely walk. Since that Mass, it is only on rare occasions that I experience that pain. Most of my focus that day was on my sixteen-year-old daughter. She didn't find a cure that night, but she survived three bouts of cancer and is now in her fifties. The spirits have told me that she has many angels that look after her. I believe they are right.

The Mass began to come to an end and Father D'Orio had begun to bless the people in wheelchairs and those who were most ill. After the service the congregants formed a line around the altar, and one by one they went up to be blessed. They would faint or fall down. At this, we decided to leave. I had seen tent services on television and wasn't so sure that it was real and not put on. Maybe the people were experiencing some form of mass hysteria. Maybe I was experiencing some type of wishful thinking. "Please cure my daughter," I thought over and over again, and then we left.

The following week I decided to go to another service with my aunt Shirley. I experienced the same feelings of awe, trepidation, and just maybe hope. Then I found out that Father D'Orio was coming to a place near where I lived in Coon Rapids, Minnesota. I had to go. I just had to. My best friend, Addie, who lived down the street from me, was the perfect person to ask. She was always up for a new adventure. I told her what had happened to me and begged her to go. "It is amazing," I said to her. "We don't really have to participate. We can just sit there and watch." Finally she agreed to go.

The night of the event arrived. I was so excited it was difficult to calm down. We arrived near the beginning of the service and had to sit in an aisle nearly at the top of the tiers of bleachers. Still, we were fairly close to the aisle and stairs leading to the altar. Father D'Orio entered from the top of the bleachers and descended to the altar directly to our left. As he came in, he stopped at the row I was sitting in and looked directly at me. I thought, "Is he looking at me? No, it can't be. There are many people in this aisle. He must be looking at someone else." Then he walked down to the altar and the Mass began.

It was the same wonderful experience as before, but even more so. Halfway through the service, Father D'Orio walked to the edge of the altar platform and looked straight up at where I was standing. Inside I gasped. "No," I said to myself, "there has to be someone else up here that he is reaching out to." I looked around to see who it could be. No one seemed to notice that I was looking at them. All eyes were on the altar. Then Father D'Orio said something about someone looking for an answer and that answer would be found that night. To this day I still believe that it had to be someone else, even though it seemed real enough that it could have been me. By this time I was shaking and doubting, and everything else in between.

The service was the same, with blessings bestowed upon the very ill and the gathering of congregants at the end. I said to my friend, "Let's go up to the altar. I've never done this before and it's his last service in Minnesota." She begrudgingly agreed.

We were in line for only a few minutes. Congregants were lined up in a circle all around the altar. One by one, Father D'Orio would bless them. Most fell down. Then it was our turn. We were at the altar waiting to get our blessing. Addie was on my right as we stood in front of the altar. Father D'Orio was coming close to us when I felt a squeeze on my left hand. I turned my head to see who had done that and there stood a Catholic nun with the most beautiful smile.

I never saw Father D'Orio come up to me or give me a blessing. I believe that when he touched me, my reaction was immediate. I was in another place that I believe was heaven. It was all white billowy clouds with a white gate of marble in the distance. There was a light coming from someone whom I couldn't see. Well, I could see him, but I couldn't make out his features. I was starting to fall down the side of the clouds. I tried with all my strength to climb up the clouds, but I couldn't. I kept falling back. I was desperate to run to the gate. I had no idea why, except for the feeling of complete euphoria.

Well, I didn't make it. I came out of my euphoria with two men pulling me up off the floor. I walked to the first row of bleachers and began to sob—I mean, really sob. My chest was heaving, tears were running down my face, and I was smiling the widest smile ever. It went on for about ten minutes, with my poor friend wondering what was happening to me. I told her, "I'm fine. I don't know why I'm crying." My entire face was covered in tears. Then it stopped and we left. I felt happier than I had in a long time.

Minneapolis and its suburbs are open all night, just like any other metropolitan city. We decided to go to a family restaurant and have coffee and a muffin. I talked nonstop all the way there.

She did not speak a word. I didn't notice. Now, this was not like either one of us. I was not a rambling talker and she was never silent.

We reached the restaurant, took a booth, and ordered coffee and a bran muffin without much fanfare. I was beginning to shut up a bit, but she was still not talking. I was still so wrapped up in what had happened to me that I really didn't notice much.

I was so thrilled by the night's occurrences. I had to find out what Addie thought, take a deep breath, stop my incessant talking, and ask her how she was. I said, "What do you think about what happened, especially at the altar?"

"I will never go into another church as long as I live."

I gasped. "What happened?" I said, stunned to the core.

"I did not have your experience. I went to someplace very frightening. There was a black cliff behind me and a black ocean in front of me and I was trapped. It was all black. Everything was black. I don't ever want to experience that again. I will never go back to another church. Never. Never again. I don't want to ever talk about this again. Let's have our coffee and go home."

I was dumbfounded. I stopped talking. I felt guilty for having taken her to the service. I don't remember if I encouraged her to go back to church, but I don't think that I did. I felt numb. It is a flashback in my memory and I will remember it always. I wonder about her often. I worry about her soul.

Clearly, I went to one place and she went to another. It is thirty years later, and as I write I remember it like it was yesterday. Her future and mine were soon to part.

I have thought many times about where heaven is. In the Lord's Prayer it says, "Our Father, who art in heaven." Okay, just where is that? Up in space? Here, all around us? Maybe in another dimension? If it was another dimension, then it could be here as well. I answered that question in the previous section in this chapter on time, but there are still more questions about heaven that I can think of. For instance, what is heaven like?

What I experienced when Father D'Orio touched me was the most awesome experience I have ever had. The euphoria was otherworldly. I am interested in near-death experiences and have several books on the subject. I have never heard of anyone having such an experience and then not believing that there is a heaven or, at the very least, a spirit world. Yet that heavenly experience appears to be different for everyone. Maybe we all have our own private heaven. After all, Christ said, "In my Father's house are many mansions."

I had a guest recently who talked about her youngest child who is now in his twenties. It seems that he has always been inclined to have accidents. She told me that when he was six years old he accidentally put his arm through a window and severed an artery. She talked with tears in her eyes even though it was now many years later. She said that the ambulance and an EMT were there in just a couple of minutes—a coincidence or something else? A woman had immediately wrapped a towel around his upper arm and stuck her hand into his arm. Blood was everywhere. In the ambulance he asked his mother if he was going to die. He did die on the operating table, but then his heart began to beat again. It was what her son told her when he came home that stunned her: "Mommy, Grandpa told me that I couldn't go to heaven yet and he sent me back here." Her father had died not too long before this incident. It was an innocent statement from a six-year-old boy.

My personal belief is that there is a personal heaven for each of us. What that awesome experience is just can't be the same for everyone. No two of us are alike.

Thousands upon thousands of people have recounted similar stories, yet science denies the existence of heaven or a spirit world. It is said that when we die our brain lights up and that what we think of as heaven is just the lights going out. People who believe that need to have a near-death experience and see for themselves! Then what will they say? Most people who are disbelievers of the spirit world will see a ghost and then say, "I didn't see anything."

Hell

Every spirit I have talked to says that there is no hell but there is a heaven that is ruled by God. I have asked each and every one of them if they have ever been to heaven. None have, but all know someone who has gone to the light, which I believe is the path to heaven. Occasionally I run across a spirit that does not know of the light.

To those of you who do not know what the light is, it is the light of God that shines down, beckoning the faithful to heaven. It is the same light that so many have seen in a near-death experience. Going to the light appears to be a different experience for everyone. I have an uncle who had a profound near-death experience. He was severely hurt in a car accident. During surgery he died. He went to the light and an entity talked to him. He said it was Jesus Christ. My uncle was told that he needed to stay on Earth to take care of his wife. That was my aunt Shirley. They ended up having seven children. The entity then said that after that task was complete he could come back. My aunt passed away in 2013. My uncle is now in the care of his son and probably waiting to see Shirley again.

I asked the spirits if Christ was going to return to Earth and rule for 3,000 years, and they said no. What they did agree upon was that God was going to return to Earth in the image of Christ.

The early settlers were Christians, as were most of the spirits at Captain Grant's. Their responses to my questions could be based on their past belief systems or not. Regardless, they are all waiting for God to return and answered saying, "It would be a good thing." Not one of them knows when that will be. Currently none of them seem to be in a hurry to go to the light. What they want to stop is being reincarnated. I have asked many spirits that accompany our guests to Captain Grant's if they are ready to go to the light. They almost always say no. They are usually waiting for the person they are watching over to die and then the two of them will go to the light and heaven together.

Oops! I didn't tell you about the spirits that follow people. Not everyone has a spirit on their shoulder, but many do. Good spirits are usually relatives who want to help guide their living loved ones to heaven. Sometimes it's a close family friend. Occasionally it's a loved one from a past life. There are times when a spirit is sent from God to watch over someone and help them. This has more to do with the spirit than with the person the spirit is guiding.

So what is heaven? Where is it? Up in the sky? In outer space? No one knows. It could be right here on Earth and all of the angels and seraphim are among us. I like that idea the best.

Well, I asked the spirits what their world was like and this is what they said. They are in the same world as us, but in a separate dimension. The spirits are the souls that God created. They are pure energy. They said that heaven is also here, but in a separate dimension from both us and the spirit world. It is hard for me to imagine a world in another dimension. My total reality is a three-dimensional Earth. I can't wrap my brain around it. In the end they stated that this dimension is time.

So what is hell? Is it fire and brimstone? Dante's inferno? Living on Earth? Well, the spirits say that there is no hell. All of them. So much for burning up in a sea of flames for eternity! What they do say is that when the evil and wicked die, their soul dies with them. They are never allowed to redeem themselves. No reincarnation for Hitler and his crew or thousands of others who reveled in the misery of others. Souls are eternal, so only God can destroy one of them. I think that it would be a matter of profound sadness for God to end the life of a soul.

Whatever or wherever heaven is, God wants us there. He has ultimate patience and watches over us through our trials and tribulations. The punishment for the truly evil is to be kept out of heaven and away from God forever. I recently asked the spirits if hell was a place devoid of light, a place of total despair where God is absent, a place of no hope. They said yes, it's an eternal abyss.

Chapter 23
THOUGHTS ABOUT SPIRITS AND COMMUNICATION METHODS

Spirits are the souls of the dead who once lived on this Earth. I have concluded that they are pure energy. If they manifest (i.e., appear as a human shape), they need to obtain more energy. They can get this energy through the electricity in a building or through a living thing, whether it be human or animal. They can also get energy through the atmosphere if there is energy present, such as during a lightning storm.

One Halloween night I was leading our guests into the cemetery across the street from my home. We all had flashlights. (I found out the year before that candles always blow out.) That afternoon my husband decided to buy all new flashlights and batteries for the night's festivities. I had the only old flashlight, but it was large and powerful.

That evening my guests and I crossed Route 2A in front of our home and entered the new Poquetanuck Cemetery. We walked about fifty feet and came to a sign designating the cemetery property. We crossed that point and every flashlight went out at the exact same time. All but mine, the only one with old batteries. For the next hour my guests walked through the cemetery in the dark unless they were near me. They even entered the underground crypt, covered with vines, without the aid of a light. When we got back to the inn, the batteries were examined and they were all dead. My husband's comment was that maybe he had bought bad batteries. That was always a possibility. But it made me wonder who had been in charge of that nighttime walk.

One time we had a ghost hunter enter the cemetery, cross the sign, take a picture, and get a tornado or vortex on her camera. It was a black funnel of air that was about five feet across on the top and narrowed to a point at the bottom. It was about six feet high. The woman stated that a vortex is where our three-dimensional world can reach the afterlife. Whether this is true or not I don't know. What I do know is that the picture was quite startling. No one caught the image with the naked eye.

We have had guests whose computer batteries have gone dead. One guest had a dead battery in his PC, but when he got home his computer worked fine and the battery was okay.

We have had many instances of the chandeliers dimming at the breakfast table, but one morning we had something quite unusual happen. We were talking about the spirits when one of the lights in one of the chandeliers became very bright and shot a beacon of light across the room. It was quite impressive and caused a flurry of conversation: "Did you see that? And did you see that?" "What was that?" "Wow." "I've never seen anything like that. Has anyone else?" And on and on for about five minutes.

Talking to the spirits can be very tiring. They take your energy in order to communicate with you. I use L-rods to communicate with the spirits. When I use the rods, the spirits are using whatever energy I am putting out there. I have seen others who can communicate with spirits and get very exhausted after they are done. This also makes me wonder what the cost is to myself to communicate with spirits. Do I really want to do this? Some call it a gift. Others call it a curse. I don't know what to call it.

Not everyone can use the rods. I have found that only a very few individuals, maybe one in fifty, can contact spirits. If you don't give off your energy for the spirits to use, they cannot communicate back to you. You may be wondering how you can learn to give off the energy. I don't think that you can learn how. You either have the ability or you don't. I can also use crystals with the same results.

One young man who stayed with us had purchased a crystal in a nearby store and was told an unlikely story. The store owner told him that the crystal would work only after he did a ritual to bring it to life. I was standing there listening to the young man and doing a slow burn. He had been duped. The crystal did not work at all for him. I asked him if he would let me hold the string that was attached to the crystal. It did what I asked. He was upset with me, thinking that I might have ruined the crystal for him. That was not the case. He simply did not have the gift. He had been ripped off.

This is what he said the store owner told him. The young man was to hold the crystal in his hands so that the crystal could get to know him. Then he was to leave the crystal in the sun for a day. He was given something to say over the crystal and then it would work. If not, try, try again.

I have also found that individuals who have had other lives are more prone to be able to use the rods. Very seldom, if ever, are new souls able to contact spirits. Now, it is not a certainty that old souls will be able to make contact either. They are just more prone to be able to do so. Only on rare occasions has a new soul, in my presence, been able to reach the spirits.

When a person uses the rods, they must be able to remain very, very still. Any activity can make the rods move. What this means is that if you want a certain outcome, you can inadvertently manipulate the rods. By doing this, you do not get accurate information. I call it a nothing session, with results caused by the person and not the spirits.

This is what I do. I sit very still, with my elbows planted on a firm surface such as a dining room table. I hold the sleeves of the rods and anchor my hands together by having my knuckles from one hand touch the knuckles of the other hand. I actually push them together. The sleeves of the rods must be free to turn at both the top and the bottom of the sleeve. Then I say a prayer.

Remember that the spirits were live people once. Treat them with respect. Tell them who you are and ask if they will talk to you. Also, instruct them on what you want the rods to do. Should they open for a yes response or close for a yes? The rods that I use are part copper and part brass. The rods that I have sold to guests are copper-clad steel. I had a guest bring rods made of metal, with the sleeves being plastic buttons. I also had a guest stay with us who had made his own rods out of clothes hangers, with a sleeve found at a plumbing store. They all worked. In ancient times willow branches were used to detect water. They were called witching rods. A willow branch with a Y at the end was used. The user would hold one part of the Y in each hand and look for water, or maybe oil if it was in the late nineteenth century. When they found the water supply, the rod would dip. If the person was using two rods, they would cross.

I had one couple stay with us who would not even consider the use of rods. They said it was not scientific. They refused to even watch a session. I say that if you are a true scientist, you will consider everything. Then you aim to disprove it. That is true science.

I still wonder if there is that certain someone out there who could prove that I am motionless when using the rods. If not, then I am unknowingly manipulating them. I talked with my husband about getting a device that holds my hands still. I have yet to find someone to test me.

Besides the rods, there is quite a bit of paraphernalia out there that can be used to detect spirits. The most common instrument that I have seen at Captain Grant's is the EVP monitor. These tiny machines record the faintest of sounds. Many voices have been captured. The first one I heard was in the upstairs hallway. A women clearly said, "Help me! Help me, please!" The little girl in the hallway who giggles, Deborah Adams, is the most often heard voice. She died at five years of age. Then of course there are the two voices that warned us of Pete.

The most frustrating occurrences for me are when I hear people talking. Once I was in one of the keeping rooms when I heard a man and woman speaking. My thought was that one of the maids had left a television on in one of the bedrooms. As I climbed the grand staircase, I could hear them but not any better than I had on the first floor. I decided the sound was coming from the Elizabeth room. I turned left and walked toward the room. When I reached the door the voices stopped. I went into the room and no one was there and the television was off. I checked each room and went back down the stairs. The voices started again. I thought that if they weren't upstairs then maybe they were in the basement. I went downstairs and talked to my sister, who was folding towels.

"Do you have a television on?" I asked her.

"No, I don't know how to turn it on," she said. My husband had jerry-rigged the television so that it was almost impossible to turn it on.

"Okay," I said. "Roberta, are you talking to yourself?" She gave me this "are you crazy?" look and I went back upstairs. After about twenty minutes the voices stopped.

Every so often I will hear my name called out, maybe about once every six months. It is usually quite loud. I call out and there is no answer, just silence. It is always when I am alone in the home. Guests have told me that they have experienced the same phenomenon. We have talked about whether this really happened or are we just a little crazy or what?

Then there are the spirits that move around when I'm preoccupied, such as when I'm in the staff bath. This week I was in the bath and heard someone walking around the house. It was quite loud. Doors opened, cabinets shut, and people walked from one end of the house to the other. "Why are the staff here?" I said to myself. "They were to be at the Avery house." Guests were to arrive there very shortly. I was irritated. I quickly left the bathroom and discovered that I was alone in the house. I called for the staff but no one answered. They were all at the Avery house. I just stood there, puzzled. "What was that? What just happened?" I called my husband and asked him if he had been in the house.

He said, "No, I'm in the workshop."

I stood there saying to myself, "Someone was here. I know they were. I know they were."

Chapter 24
CAMERAS AND APPARITIONS

It is common for our guests to get pictures of orbs, fog, ghosts, and unexplainable images. Hundreds of pictures have been taken in the Grant home, plus hundreds more outside and in the two cemeteries.

The most common of these pictures feature orbs. An orb is a round light image that appears on a camera's picture. It can be large or small. I took a picture in the attic of an orb that was at least two feet in diameter. They can also be just a couple of inches across. Most of them have designs on them that remind me of Celtic circles. On rare occasions they will have a face. A guest of ours filmed in the Adelaide room and got an orb coming out of the ceiling by the bathroom. It went to a picture of a ship that I have on the wall, went between the glass, and the picture and moved back and forth over the ship. It then flew off the picture and through the glass, then went across the room and back up into the attic.

One morning after breakfast in the dining room (we sometimes eat outside), a guest took a picture of everyone sitting around the table. We had spent about an hour discussing spirits. Lo and behold, the camera had captured ten orbs of different sizes floating above the table—big ones, small ones, all sizes.

Orbs were captured in these photos a guest took in the game room.
Photo credit: Joanna Bagarella

Orbs appeared in every photo this family took during their stay at Captain Grant's. Photo credit: Rebecca Abrams

In the south cemetery known as Cemetery #17, there is an orb that appears as bright orange or sometimes red and at other times as bright yellow. It has been captured by several cameras but has also been seen with the naked eye. I keep thinking it has to be a light from somewhere, but I don't know where that somewhere would be. Behind the cemetery is a short cliff, a stream below that, and then woods—nothing else. I have seen this orb on several occasions. I have walked into the meadow and stared at the red orb. No one is there. Nothing is there. I have questioned my neighbors, but they don't know what it is either. It's just a round red light that is sometimes yellow and is really not there. Although this phenomenon is round, it is probably a different entity altogether and not a true orb. Guests have recorded that the light seemed to follow them. I won't go into the cemetery at night. There are graves that have sunk into the ground, with only a few inches remaining above the ground. The graves are not in even rows, and if you don't have good light you could fall. There are also more graves with headstones leaning over than standing up straight.

One of the most interesting orbs I've seen was captured outside the house at night. It was sitting on top of Captain Grant's and had to be at least three feet in diameter. And, no, it was not the moon. The moon was in another section of the sky. The size of this orb was phenomenal, to say the least. It was captured on film and then poof, it was gone.

Debunkers don't believe that there are orbs or that orbs are the souls of spirits. They have thrown dust in the air and have gotten dust orbs on pictures. Dust orbs and spirit orbs are quite different entities. You can also get orbs with water thrown into the air. Spirit orbs are captured on film in unlikely places. Take the one on our roof. How did that get up there and what about the size? It was huge. Also, consider the orb that passed through the picture to be under the glass and over the ship. While under the glass, it moved back and forth and then shot through the glass to the other side of the room. I strongly believe that orbs are the souls of those who have passed out of this world and into the next. For the scientists out there, how can you make a bit of dust go under a picture and then through glass?

Pictures of fog and mist have also been taken on the property. I find them very interesting. They do not look exactly like fog. There is a shape to them somewhat like looking up at clouds. At Captain Grant's, the usual places to find fog are on the first-floor deck where we have breakfast in the morning or in the old cemetery behind the house. You can't see this fog with the naked eye, but only with a camera. Guests who have taken several pictures in a row have captured the fog and then in the next frame it's gone. Before starting this journey with spirits, I had never heard of a "fog." Maybe this is the "mist" some people describe, only there was not a dampness in the air when the pictures were taken and I believe a mist would feel damp. It is truly amazing to look at the edge of your deck, in a picture, and see something as total fog when you were unable to see it with your naked eye.

A series of photos taken in the cemetery near Captain Grant's (continued on next page).

*A series of photos taken in the cemetery near Captain Grant's.
The mist wasn't visible to the naked eye.
Photo credits: Dennis and Carrie Lowe*

The big question is, why can the camera capture the image but we cannot see it with the naked eye? My husband has a theory about this. The human eye can see only a certain width on the spectrum of light. The camera must be able to see just a bit wider on that spectrum than we can.

It is not just cameras but also some dogs, cats, and humans who have this ability. Are they able to see just a bit wider width, as well as a camera can? This is a theory that is worth exploring. Science could study spectrum widths with people known to be able to see spirits. They could also study spectrum widths with cats and dogs. Do they match the spectrum widths of cameras? This is a challenge to all of those scientists out there that say there are no ghosts.

What about the people who see ghosts on rare occasions? I am one of them. As I recounted earlier, I saw my first and my second spirit in my early thirties. I was living in Coon Rapids, Minnesota, in my first haunted house. The two spirits that I saw were most likely the same spirit. The first time I saw him he was on top of our bedroom chest of drawers. I was sitting up in bed waiting for my husband when an orb appeared above the chest of drawers. Then it grew a body and legs. I remember that my mouth was wide open and I was staring. "Holy smoke!" I said to myself. I called out to my husband and as soon as I did, it shriveled up, its head going last.

The next time I saw this spirit was about a year later. I was reading a book at the kitchen table. My husband was standing next to me. I knew he wanted to go to bed and was in a hurry for me to put the book down. Then I heard my husband call my name from the other side of the house and ask me when I was coming to bed. I froze. I looked sideways and he vanished.

That house was seriously haunted. We couldn't get babysitters, and everyone who stayed with us told us we had a ghost. Friends and relatives would come over to visit and say, "Did you know that you have a ghost in this house?" My mother-in-law told me that we had a ghost. She was a devout Catholic and would never have said such a thing unless she really believed it. We bought the home from a widow who lost her husband in a tragic motorcycle accident. I think that the spirit could have been that man.

My third experience with seeing a ghost was at Captain Grant's. It was after a big breakfast. The inn was full with guests that day. The staff were at the Avery house (where we live) cleaning rooms, and my husband had just gone to his workshop. I was alone.

If you are in the kitchen of Captain Grant's, you have a clear line of sight through the house going through the kitchen, dining room, and keeping room. I looked through into the keeping room and saw a man with dark hair and wearing black pants and a white shirt walk toward the front door. I called out. No answer. I called out again. No answer. Then I called for my husband. "Ted, are you here?" No answer. I went to see who was there, and of course there was no one.

We had a young maid named Amie who had a child spirit walk through her. We had another staff member see a woman dressed in colonial garb on the stairs, and several guests have seen a woman and two children in the Adelaide room. A few of our guests have drawn pictures of what they saw.

Amie, our maid, had been straightening a metal mini blind in the Adelaide bathroom. Her arms were stretched out in front of her when a little girl walked through them. Amie was inconsolable. We sent her home, where she stayed for three days, too scared to come back to work.

My point is, why can some people see spirits and then not be able to see them? Why can some of us see spirits only at intervals? We are not the individuals who can see beyond the usual spectrum of light. We are the people in between. Someone once called me a sensitive. Maybe those of us who see the spirits occasionally indeed are sensitives. The spirits told me that a sensitive has the ability to give off energy. That makes it possible for spirits to manifest. They have to have energy to manifest fully. Individuals who always can see in a wider spectrum of light would be able to see spirits at any time.

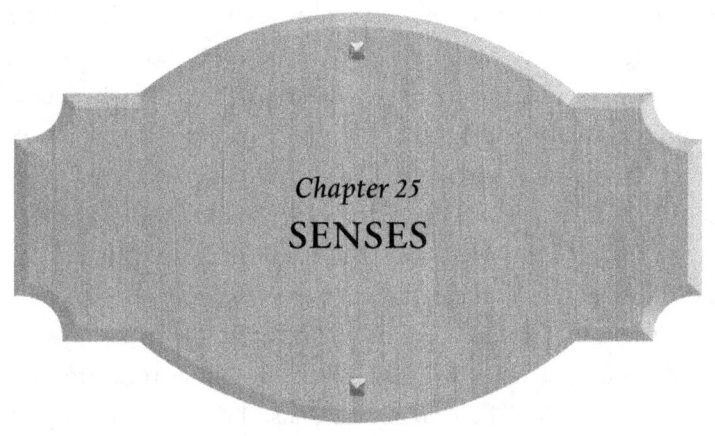

Chapter 25
SENSES

The five senses of hearing, touch, smell, sight, and taste give us the data we need to make sense of our world. Everything we know comes from one of those senses. When it comes to senses and the spirits, humans are not at all alike. Some of us can use one of the senses to a great extent, but others cannot. Some of us use more than one sense to detect a ghostly presence, and a very privileged few can use all five.

Then there is the sixth sense we call intuition. I believe that intuition is using the five senses but on a level that we are not aware of. Our brain catalogs a lot of information that we can piece together to give us logical answers to the mysteries around us in a nanosecond of time.

So what do the different individuals who use different senses say about their experiences with the spirit world? Here are descriptions of some of my own experiences as well as recollections of what dozens of my guests have told me about this issue.

Hearing

I happen to be one of those people who hears ghosts. This has been occurring since I was a small child. I would hear boots coming up the stairs at night. I would lay in bed and wonder why whoever was coming up the stairs never made it to the top but just kept on coming up. I also wondered why my parents didn't go and see who was there. By the time I was ten years old or so I knew that there was no one there. When I left home I didn't hear those footsteps again until I was in my sixties, and then I only heard them once.

At Captain Grant's, I hear people talking. This is mainly a man and a woman. That is all I can make out. What they are saying is not discernible. Their voices have also been captured by EVP equipment on many occasions.

Guests also tell me of a child who giggles in the hallway at night. It is usually just one guest who reports this, even if there are ten or more people staying in the house. If it had been only one guest one time who said there was giggling, I would dismiss it. However, this is not the case. Over the years many guests have reported hearing the little girl giggle.

The most amazing thing that has to do with sound was heard by a family who stayed in the Collette room. During the day the father sat on the second-floor deck reading to his daughter. The story he was reading was about an Indian boy and his drum. The father held his daughter on his lap while he read to her. I saw them through the hallway door. It was a very loving picture for my memories.

The next morning the father came to talk to me. Either he or he and his wife were woken up in the wee hours of the morning while it was still dark outside. Above the twin bed, where their little girl lay, was the sound of a drum drumming at a slow beat. His daughter was sitting there listening with a big smile.

What makes these sounds heard by a few people and not everyone? What about the "sometimes" factor, such as on those rare occasions when my husband can also hear what I am hearing? This has occurred when the noise has been quite loud. It could have been talking or a disturbance of some sort, such as loud knocking on the front door. The most common thing that my husband and I hear are the two people talking in the Holly room while we are upstairs in the office. There are also other sounds that come from that room.

In my case, I am almost deaf in one ear. This should limit what I can hear, but it does not. Can some of us detect a sound frequency that others can't hear? Something like the sounds that dogs can hear but not humans? We still don't have equipment good enough to capture audibly what is said. There is a lot of guessing about what is actually said on an EVP monitor.

My views on clairaudience have changed somewhat since I began writing this book. I have met so many people who can hear the spirits, including my skeptic husband, that I now believe everyone has this capability.

Touch

For about three years, three women came and stayed at Captain Grant's. They were a mother and her two daughters. They stayed in the Collette room, where there are two beds. The sisters slept in the queen bed and the mother slept in the twin bed. The mother was in her mid-seventies. What struck me most about her was her intelligence. She had been a professor of ancient history and loved to share stories about the Middle East. Every time these three stayed at Captain Grant's, the mother was touched by a spirit. This did not happen to her at other locations. She described the touch as a brushing of her cheek. She began to expect that this was going to happen whenever she stayed at Captain Grant's.

Other guests have talked about being able to actually feel a presence. One man described going down a hallway that wasn't lit and bumping into someone. He turned to apologize but there was no one there. Another guest spoke of being grabbed by the arm. He told the spirit, "Let go of me." Then the sensation of being grabbed was gone.

Guests also speak about having someone sit on them in bed. Sometimes they get poked. This is quite a common event. I consider that the sensation of pressure against the body. I had a dearly loved Siamese cat that talked to me on a regular basis. In fact, he talked all the time. One day he disappeared. I sometimes feel the pressure of his paws on my bed at night. I feel the jump onto the bed and then the walking toward the head of the bed. He always slept on my head, but the sensation never gets that far. It stops at about waist level.

When guests tell me that they "feel" something, I don't consider it the same as actually feeling pressure against the body. I believe that the emotion of feeling something has to do with the senses picking up information. In this case the person is not attuned to their senses in such a way that they recognize what is happening to them. It just comes out as "I feel a presence is here." In this case, if the person were to pay more attention to what is going on with themselves, they might be able to become more astute at knowing when a spirit is present.

My husband and I now have a new spirit in our bedroom. The spirit pushes me. Twice he pushed my elbow hard enough to move my arm forward. Once he pushed my shoulder. I was lying in bed waiting to get into the bathroom. When I felt the shove I said, "Okay, I'll get up." I thought that my husband was behind me.

Sight

Being able to see ghosts is truly a special gift. This happens to some of us on rare occasions, but for others it is on a regular basis. Sometimes spirits will appear to someone. By this I mean that they will materialize in our three-dimensional world. The spirit needs a great deal of energy to do this.

For individuals who can see spirits at will, are they seeing them in the spirits' world? I don't think that is the case. I believe they are seeing them in our three-dimensional world even if the spirit is only two-dimensional. Their form has no substance, no depth. But it has height and width, which is actually two-dimensional. So how do the spirits take on form? They need energy. Individuals who can see spirits on an ongoing basis must give off enough energy for the spirit to take form. Now that is an awesome feat! How can they do that? Most people believe it is all hocus pocus and make-believe. But then what about the children who see spirits and dogs that growl at the air or cats that try to claw the air? Truly they must be looking at something. Also, are they giving off energy on a regular basis?

For the young children who see spirits, many of them apparently lose this ability as they become adults. What happens to them? Does the more rational mind of an adult subdue their ability to see what others can't? Does the adult worry about being thought of as different? Or does the child change physically in some way that does not allow them to see the spirits any longer as an adult?

We have had dozens of ghost hunters and ghost-seeking groups stay at the bed and breakfast. Most are young and ghost hunting is just a passing fad for them. However, a few of the groups are scientific in their approach to finding evidence of spirit presence. One of these groups spent time talking about theories of what is going on with individuals who can see spirits.

One theory is that these individuals who can see ghosts received a strong electric shock as a child. Although the guest said that there is a strong correlation between receiving an electric shock and being able to see spirits, it is not 100 percent. For instance, I could hear a ghost when I was a child but I didn't have a bad electric shock until I was in my twenties. However, this theory may be worth pursuing.

Another theory is genetics. I have met many guests who have abilities and so did other members of their family, especially in past generations. If it is genetic, then we should ask ourselves, what is it that is different about those families?

Smell and Taste

Different smells are said to mean different things. The smell of roses is said to be a "good" smell. It could be a loving relative or a person unknown to us. The aroma of rotten eggs, on the other hand, is said to represent an evil presence. One evening I had a very strong scent of a man who had abused me many years earlier. Were my old fears of this man conjuring up his scent, or was it something else?

Smell and taste work closely together. It is not at all uncommon for someone to smell something offensive and then taste it in their mouth. Smelling lemons can make the mouth pucker.

I am not sure what role these two senses play in recognizing that a spirit is nearby, but I believe that they do. They may be overshadowed by the other three senses. The sense of smell is the strongest one we have in being attracted to another person. We are mostly unaware of this and instead say, "I really like the way he looks" or "His voice is so sexy." The attraction is to the other person's pheromones, not to their perfume. Every individual has a particular smell. This is why people will say, "I smelled my grandfather last night." The man had his own particular smell that was recognized by his grandchild.

At Captain Grant's, I am glad to say that we seem to almost have an absence of smells other than from living sources in our world. Only the Collette and Margaret rooms have occasionally had a smell. That was of lilacs and also lavender, which were popular fragrances in the past. Just this morning I detected the strong scent of flowers as I went into the basement. The Margaret room smells of pipe tobacco at different times of the year.

There needs to be more research done in this area. It could prove quite useful.

CONCLUSION

Over the years I have learned that the more I know, the more I don't know. One bit of knowledge leads to another question, and so on and so forth. In the time that I have owned Captain Grant's, my life has taken dramatic turns. My belief system has been hit hard with new truths. I have had to look at my past and accept that I was not always in charge. What I do have is a strong belief in my faith. That has led me to look at what I have learned about the paranormal as stemming from a higher power. I also believe that most individuals accept that there is a higher power. We don't all agree on just what or who that is. My beliefs about the paranormal don't always match those of other researchers, but that is research. We keep going until we have the truth.

I continue to run Captain Grant's with my husband Tadashi. Paranormal events occur on almost a daily basis. Most of these are not worth mentioning. There may be a tap at a guest's door when no one is there or a depression in the mattress while someone is in bed.

Maybe a statue is found in a different room from where it should be. Our guests are usually very satisfied with what they experience. For many it is just orbs. Only on rare occasions will a guest be angry that they didn't have an experience. Most of those who still haven't had a paranormal experience plan to come back and hope to have one in the future.

The bed and breakfast is like a big family. We've seen people get engaged, get married, and then have children who grow up and go to college. We have been at this for twenty-two years. The spirits that surround us have begun to feel like friends. Even our repeat guests will ask about Adelaide or Deborah Adams. Neither my husband nor I have ever been afraid of the spirits. We have shaken our heads in disbelief, looked for explanations when there were none, and kept quiet when a guest has a Hollywood belief in the afterlife—the "Friday the Thirteenth" sort of useless knowledge that only scares people and leads nowhere. It is entertaining for those who like to be scared out of their wits.

I still continue to hold ghost communication lessons if a guest requests one. It is a gift that I have and I enjoy sharing it. I have conquered my hesitation in talking about the spirits. I listen to myself and say, "You really believe in what you have learned." And I do.

Tadashi and I are going to continue to run Captain Grant's. We enjoy our guests (family) and spend as much time as we can with them. The spirit world is the hottest topic of conversation around the breakfast table. It even beats politics.

I have learned a lot from psychics, sensitives, and many other individuals who know there is another world out there that we can't see. I enjoy spending time with them and hearing their views.

Most of them agree on what I have shared with them about the bed and breakfast, often saying, "You are right. I sense that as well."

Now, in my later years, I know that my life has been guided by spirits.

Appendix
SPIRIT INTERVIEWS

This appendix contains close-to-verbatim conversations I have had with the spirits at Captain Grant's and the Avery home.

Interview with Deborah Adams

"Hello. It is Carol again. Could I speak with Deborah?" After a lot of rod swinging, they finally settled down. "Deborah, is it you?"

"Yes." The rods opened wide and one rod touched my face. That is a hugging gesture. Deborah often touches both of my cheeks in a gesture of happiness.

"I want to write about you. I would like to know if it would be okay with you if I put you in a book."

"Yes."

"Deborah, you were five years old when you died of an illness. Are you still five years old?"

"No."

"Does your spirit age?"

"Yes."

"Deborah, have you lived another life before you were Deborah?"
"Yes."
"Was it in the 1600s?"
"No."
"Was it in the 1500s?"
"Yes."
"Were you a woman then?"
"Yes."
"Did you have children?"
"Yes."
"Did you do something bad that you had to atone for?"
"Yes."
"Is that why you are here now as Deborah Adams?"
"Yes."
"Deborah, do you think your soul will be reborn into another living human being? Do you think that you will come back?"
"No."
"Do you know other souls that you have lived with when you were alive?"
"Yes."
"Have you ever met anyone in the spirit world that you knew when you were alive?"
"No."

I was very surprised at this. I have heard so many stories of people seeing their loved ones in near-death experiences. I decided to probe a little deeper.

"Do you remember your mother?"
"Yes."
"Do you remember your father?"
"Yes."
"Did your mother live to be old?"

"No."

I found out from several questions that Deborah was the third child but not the last. So if her mother had had other children after Deborah, her mother must have died shortly after that or perhaps in childbirth later on.

"After your parents died, did you see them in the spirit world?"
"No."
"Are they also buried in the cemetery behind the house?"
"Yes."
"Are their spirits in this house?"
"No."
"Deborah, did your parents go toward a bright light?"
"Yes."

At this point in the interview, I changed course a bit. I planned to come back to the white light toward the end of our conversation.

"When I asked you this morning if you could come next door with me to my office, you said no. Then I asked you if you could ever leave this house and you said no. Is this true?"
"Yes."
"Deborah, is your spirit trapped in this house?"
"Yes."
"Have you ever wanted to leave or be reborn?"
"No."
"Do you like being a spirit?"
"Yes."
"Do you like living people being around you?"
"Yes."
"Sometimes our guests hear a little girl giggling. Is that you?"
"Yes."
"Are you playing with another child spirit that is also in this house?"

"Yes."

"I don't know the other child's name. Is it a boy?"

I have had guests tell me that a little boy spirit is also in the house, so that was my first thought when asking this question.

"Yes."

"Was he alive when you were alive?"

"No."

"Would you please point the rods toward where he is buried?"

Slowly the rods turned until both of them were pointing at the cemetery across the street. This cemetery was established in 1903. The male child had to have lived sometime in the late nineteenth or the early twentieth century. I then told Deborah that I would like to talk to him at a later time. At this, the rods just went back and forth.

"Deborah, do you continue to learn from our world as your spirit goes on?"

"Yes."

"So that is how you can answer questions that most five-year-olds can't. Do you want to be in this house forever?"

"Yes."

"Do you see a bright light? It is the one your parents went to. I had an experience once where I was in the clouds and was very happy. Have you ever seen a light or had an experience like mine?"

"No."

"Do you see the light?" I said with emphasis.

"Yes."

I talked to Deborah for a while after that. I told her that she should not be afraid of the light. I asked one favor of her and that was if she planned to go to the light to tell Daniel to tell me that she had gone. She agreed.

Interview with Daniel

I sat in the kitchen and asked the spirits if Daniel could speak to me. The rods answered with a wide-apart yes.

"Daniel, are you related to Samuel?"

"Yes."

"Are you his son?"

"Yes."

"Was your father a farmer?"

The rods crossed. "No."

This surprised me since Preston was and currently is a farming community and Samuel's family had so much land.

"Was your father a blacksmith?" I had been told a few years prior that the home next door to Captain Grant's was a blacksmith shop at one time. Supposedly the front of the building, which had been a blacksmith shop, had actually been built in the 1600s but had experienced a fire at some point in time and then was rebuilt into a home in 1790. Then in 1817 an addition was added onto the back of the small home.

"Yes."

I asked him for a house number but got a number that I doubt was ever a blacksmith shop. Possibly they didn't have numbered houses in the 1700s or they were different than the numbers we use today.

"I am going to ask you how old you were when you died." I began by asking if he was over 30.

"No."

Then I went to over 25.

"No."

"Over 20?"

"Yes."

"Were you 21 when you died?"
"Yes."
"Was it an accident?"
"Yes."
"At your father's shop?"
"Yes."
"Did you ever marry?"
"No."
"Did you ever father children?"
"Yes."
"More than one?"
It turned out to be two children.
"Was the mother's family name Avery?"

Avery is another famous village name. One of the roads close by to Captain Grant's is named Avery Hill.

"Yes."
"Did your parents approve of her?"
"No."
"Did your parents ever accept the children as their grandchildren?"
"No."
"Did they know that you had children?"
"No."
"Do you know who your descendants are?"
"Yes."
"Do you watch them?"
"Yes."
"Would you like to come back, be reborn?"
"No."
"Do you see a light?"
"Yes."

"You don't go to this light?"
"No."
"Do you want to go?"
"No."
"Do you want to stay in this house forever?"

The rods wavered back and forth and then he said yes. It appeared that he was not sure of what he wanted to do.

I told him, "This house won't stand forever. Eventually it will come down."

Then I changed the subject a bit.

"Daniel, do you communicate with the other spirits in the house?"
"Yes."
"What are spirits? Are you energy?"
"Yes."
"Are you the souls of people who have died?"
"Yes."
"Has your soul lived in another human being before it was in Daniel?"
"Yes."
"More than one other life?"
"Yes."
"More than two?"
"No."

So it was determined that Daniel was in his third life when he lived at Captain Grant's. If he died at 21, he might not have lived long enough to resolve whatever issues needed to be resolved from his past life.

"Daniel, are you going to be reborn again?"
"Yes."
"Do you have a choice in the matter?"

"No."

"Can you pick who you will be reborn into?"

"No."

"Does God do all of the choosing?"

"Yes."

At this point it became clear why Daniel can't go to the light. He has to be reincarnated.

"Do you have something to atone for while you were alive?"

"Yes."

"When you go into this newborn child, is it at the conception of that child?"

"No."

"Is it at the instant of birth?"

"Yes."

"Do you know when it will happen?" Meaning, when will he be reborn?

"No."

"In helping my guests determine whether they have ever lived before, it seems that reincarnation happens most often about every two to three hundred years. Is this correct?"

"Yes."

"So this could happen to you at any time."

"Yes."

"With no warning?"

"Yes."

Again I changed the subject to find out more information.

"Daniel, do you know if souls that have gone to the light ever come back?"

"No."

"When I talk to you, do I give you the energy to move the rods?"

"Yes."

"Most people can't communicate with spirits. Is it because they don't give off enough energy?"

"Yes."

"Can they learn to give energy to the spirits?"

"No."

"Can you get energy from electronics?"

"Yes."

"I have heard that people who have had an electric shock can sometimes become able to communicate with spirits. Is this true?"

"Yes."

"Daniel, I need to make my husband some supper. The time is getting late. I will talk to you at another time."

The rods swung back and forth. Then both rods came up to my cheeks and gave me a hug. It was hard to let him go.

It was now Sunday morning. All night I had tossed and turned. Daniel's story was missing something. In the 1700s a young woman with two illegitimate children would be scorned by the entire community. Why couldn't he marry her? Because his parents didn't approve. No. They didn't know her. That didn't make sense. When a man got a woman pregnant they were forced to wed immediately. Shotgun weddings they called it, and they continued into the 1900s. I had to go back and talk to him again.

That afternoon I again picked up the rods and contacted Daniel.

"Daniel, I would like to ask you more questions about your children and their mother. Is that okay with you?"

"Yes."

"Daniel, you couldn't marry this woman. Was she a close relative?"

"No."

"Was she married to another man?"

"Yes."

"Did her husband ever find out?"

With this question the rods slowly swung back and forth.

"You don't know?"

Daniel finally affirmed that her husband did not know.

"Would she lay with him?"

"No."

"Was he abusive? Did he hurt her?"

"Yes."

With this answer I thought that Daniel was a bit naive. If her husband didn't lie with her, then he would have known that the two children his wife had were not his. Someone was not telling the truth. My guess was that this women laid with her husband and was too frightened or ashamed to tell Daniel.

Since that interview, I have thought about trying to trace Daniel's lineage and see if there are any ties to the Averys. Perhaps I could find an Avery family that had two children and lived at the same time as Daniel did. Maybe the woman would be around Daniel's age. It seems that the more I delve into the spirits' lives, the more questions I have.

First Interview with Mercy Adelaide Grant

"Mercy, I am writing a book and I want to have a chapter dedicated to you. Is this okay with you?"

"Yes."

"I have a quick question for you and then I have to tend to the B&B business. Can you come to my office next door for the interview?"

"Yes."

"You're not trapped in this house?"

"No."

"Great."

It was now Saturday, six days after I last communicated with Mercy. It turned out that she had been following me to my office ever since I had asked if she could do that. For myself, this was the most interesting session with a spirit that I had ever had. In fact, it was a little too interesting and I'm not certain that I believe what Mercy told me. You be the judge.

"I have a bit of time to talk to Mercy. Are you here with me?"
"Yes."
"You are buried across the street. Is this correct?"
"Yes."
"There is a grave next to you. Does that belong to your husband?"
"No."
"Does it belong to your son who was also named William Grant?"
"Yes."
"Did you live a long life?"
"Yes."
"Did you die in your eighties?"
"No."

I was very surprised at this answer. I had believed that she had died in her 80s ever since the remaining Grant family visited us in 1995. After going through the seventies, sixties, fifties, forties, thirties, and twenties, I decided to go up and not down.

"Mercy did you die in your nineties?"
"Yes."

We finally got ninety-three years by using the same method of asking for each year.

"Mercy, the Captain died at age thirty-two. Did you ever remarry?"

"No."

"Did you stay in the home after he died?"

"No."

"Did you sell the big house?"

"No."

"The Captain also owned the home next door and the home across the street. Is this correct?"

"Yes."

"Did you sell those homes?"

"Yes."

"Did you move to Colchester after that?"

"Yes."

I had previously been told that descendants of Captain Grant now reside in Colchester, so it was a logical question for me to ask.

"Did your family help you after the Captain's death?"

"Yes."

I wanted to know more about Mercy on the spirit level so I changed the subject.

"Mercy, you have been in this house a very long time. Do you see a light?"

"Yes."

"You don't want to go to the light?"

"No."

"Can you go to the light?"

"Yes."

"Are you waiting for the Captain?"

"Yes."

"Can I help you get him here?"

"No."

"Mercy, have you lived other lives?"

"Yes."

"More than two?"
"Yes."
"Three?"
"Yes."
"Has the Captain also led other lives?"
"Yes."

Then I got the idea that maybe he had been reborn again and she was waiting for him to die. "That is why she won't leave," I said to myself. There was a real chance that they could be together again.

"Has he been reincarnated since he died?"
"Yes."
"So if he has been reincarnated, are you now waiting for him to die again?"
"Yes."
"Does he live in Preston?" Preston is the town where Captain Grant's bed and breakfast is located. Poquetanuck is a village inside the town.

The rods wavered back and forth. Then I remembered that Mercy would have called the town Poquetanuck.

"Does he live in Poquetanuck?"
"Yes."

At this my heart started to pound. Neighbors in that town don't socialize on a regular basis. In fact, if it isn't through church or a town function, they rarely get together. So if I know this man, it would be one of very few men.

"Do I know him?"
"Yes."
"Mercy, is Captain Grant's soul in my husband Ted [Tadashi]?"
"Yes."
"Oh God," I thought. "This is crazy."

"Mercy, when I bought Captain Grant's, there was a very high possibility that I would fail. I only had $112 in the bank after closing and this house was falling apart, but one miracle after another began happening. Did the other spirits in the house help you to help me?"

"Yes."

"You wanted me here."

"Yes."

"Do the spirits communicate with each other?"

"Yes."

"So you knew that Captain Grant's soul was in my husband and you brought Ted [number two] here and we got married." It all sounded a little too bizarre to comprehend. I had to talk to Ted and tell him about this session. My mind was racing and I could no longer concentrate. I had to move on to another subject. It was truly a miracle that I had Captain Grant's. I had always felt that I had help from St. Anthony. Now I didn't know what to believe. "No, it had to be St. Anthony," I said to myself.

"Mercy, would you answer some questions about souls, reincarnation, and God?"

"Yes."

"Does God send the souls back to be reincarnated?"

"Yes."

"Is that so they can work out their mission on Earth?"

"Yes."

"Does God want all of the souls in heaven?"

"Yes."

"Will everyone get to go to heaven?"

"No."

"Will the wicked and evil get into heaven?"

"No."

"Will they go to hell?"

"No."

I was surprised at her answer and sat and thought for a few minutes. I asked myself, "Where do they go?" They don't go to heaven. They don't go to hell. Then a possibility came to me.

Mercy, when the evil and wicked die, do their souls die with them?"

"Yes."

"But those of us who make bad decisions but are not evil or wicked get another chance and are reborn until we get it right?"

"Yes."

"Will Jesus Christ come back as prophesy dictates?"

"No."

"Will God come back to Earth?"

"Yes."

"Will he come back in the form of Jesus Christ?"

"Yes."

"Do you know when it will happen?"

A large crossing of the rods occurred, making her answer a definite no.

We talked a little longer about religions and beliefs of people around the world. I asked her about all of the major religions. She had answers for all of my questions. What I still don't know is if this knowledge is from her own belief system when she was a live human being or things that her soul learned after her death. Regardless, her answers were too hot to handle.

Two months passed and I had read this interview a dozen times or more. A couple of things stood out as being non-truths. When Mercy stated that she was waiting for my husband to die so that she and the Captain could go to the light together, it went against something one of the spirits had said to me earlier. I will take Daniel as the example. When Daniel died, his spirit remained Daniel. He did not revert to the person he was before Daniel. Of course this would mean that when my husband dies, his spirit will remain him. He will not become Captain Grant and go to the light with Mercy.

Then I got a visit from none other than Captain Grant's descendants. My husband and I talked to them for several minutes. I asked them if any of their relatives had ever moved to Colchester. They said that the family had migrated to Lisbon, Connecticut, and were adamant that no Grant had ever lived in Colchester. They also said that Captain Grant had been buried in the cemetery across the street and not at sea.

Now the dilemma. It seemed obvious that Mercy was lying. After another month of thinking about this, I came to a conclusion about what had gone wrong with the interview. When I interviewed Mercy, it was next door where my office is. That house also has two spirits. Could it be that one of those spirits answered as Mercy? I decided to take my rods and do the interview over at Captain Grant's.

Second Interview with Mercy Adelaide Grant

"Mercy, I did an interview with you about three months ago. Do you remember?"

"Yes."

"It was in my office next door. Did one of the spirits in that house answer for you?"

"Yes."

"Is it better for us to have a meeting in the big house?"

"Yes."

"Did any of Captain Grant's descendants ever live in Colchester?"

"No."

"Did your descendants live in Colchester?"

"Yes."

"Did you live in the big house until your death?"

"Yes."

"Is the Captain buried at sea?"

"Yes."

She never changed her stance on that question even though the descendants had said otherwise.

"Did you live into your eighties?"

"Yes."

The questions continued and the situation taught me a lesson or rather reminded me of what I already knew. You can't see who you are talking to or be able to tell if they are telling the truth or lying.

I believe the real Mercy is the one I communicated with in the big house.

Before leaving Mercy, I decided to ask her a few more questions about reincarnation and manifestation.

"Mercy, I have some questions about manifestation. There are many ghost hunters that come to Captain Grant's to investigate spirits. They all say that it is easier to manifest at night. Is this the truth?"

"No."

"Is it just as easy to manifest during the day?"

"Yes."

Perhaps it is easier for a person to see them at night because they are energy and give off light. During daylight the energy that is manifested may be difficult for the human eye to capture.

"Mercy, I now have some questions about reincarnation. Can you be reincarnated back into the same person you were and relive your life over again?"

"No."

"Can you be reborn to a previous time?"

"No."

"So the soul always goes forward in time?"

"Yes."

"I am a Christian and was told that we only live one life. Is this true?"

"Yes."

"Then my conclusion is that it is the soul that continues to come back and not the person. Is this right?"

"Yes."

"If the soul is reincarnated, it can come back to parents that live anywhere on Earth. It could also be of either sex and of any race. Is this correct?"

"Yes."

When I do ghost communication lessons with guests, quite often the reincarnated person, or soul, is of a different race, from a different country, or of the opposite sex. This can be quite disappointing for some real macho men who find out that the last time around they were a woman. Of course that woman died and her soul went on.

I believe that when God reincarnates a soul, it is for that soul to complete its purpose on Earth. That being said, perhaps the purpose is better fulfilled in another place, in another gender, or in another race. Maybe all three. "Mercy, do you believe there could be some truth in that?"

"Yes."

Then came a question that I didn't wish to ask Mercy. It is between you, the reader, and me. Given all that I have gotten from Mercy, it appears that a soul may have lived many times, occupying several different people. In that case, when God returns as Christ, are we reborn or are the souls reborn? If there is one soul for three people, who is reborn?

Interview with Liam

I started the interview focusing on Liam being gay.

"Liam, were men prosecuted for being attracted to men when you were alive?"

"No."

"Did you ever have a male lover? A man that you loved?"

"Yes."

"Did he love you?"

"Yes."

"Do you think God loves you even though you loved a man and not a woman?"

"Yes."

"Does God care that you loved a man?"

"No."

The rods slowly waved back and forth. It was as if Liam was wondering why I would ask these questions. I felt as if I were talking to an innocent.

"Liam, do you know your last name?"

"Yes."

"Do you mind if I find out what it is?"

"No."

At this, I went through the alphabet and came up with a G for the first letter of his last name. I asked him if he was a Geer, and he said yes. The Geer family is one of the original families of the village. They have a monument in the old cemetery.

My intuition said, "This is too easy. Something is amiss." I decided to take the interview in another direction and talk about reincarnation.

"Liam, did you have any other lives before you were Liam?"

"Yes."

We went through the one, two, three, and four routine I had developed and got three other lives for Liam.

"Were you ever a woman?"

"Yes."

"More than one time?"

"No."

"Did you ever have children?"

"No."

"Do you think that you will be reborn again?"

"Yes."

"Is that because you never had children?"

"Yes."

"So you need to come back and have children?"

"Yes."

"Liam, do you believe in God?"

"Yes."

"Do you think the Antichrist is on Earth?"

"Yes."

There it was again. An answer that was too pat. When I get an instant turn of the rods, they are answering that they clearly know the answer. If it is a tougher question, the rods may waver back and forth a bit prior to answering. With that, the answer they give might still be wrong.

I decided to go through the continents with Liam and ended up with Asia as the continent where the Antichrist is. Then I went through Asian countries and ended up with India. "No way," I said to myself. "There is a problem with this interview."

"Liam, are you playing a game with me?"

"Yes."

"Has any of what you have told me been the truth?"

"No."

"Liam, I need to go. I'll talk to you tomorrow."

The rods flew back and forth and went around like helicopter blades. Liam did not want to end the conversation. He was having a good time being a tease.

I had to sleep on this interview. Were they all lying to me or just Liam? With no facial features or personal clues to go on, I was at a standstill.

I ended up waiting three days before going back to talk to Liam. I sat at the kitchen table in the bed and breakfast, took out my rods, and began.

"Liam, hi. It's me, Carol, again. Are you here?"

"Yes."

"Are you happy to see me?"

"Yes."

"I would like to know your last name. Is it Geer?"

"No."

"Okay. Let's try again. Please tell me the truth this time. Does your name start with an A?"

"No."

Then I went on to B, C, and D, all of the way through to Z. I sat and thought for a minute. My iced tea was in front of me, so I decided to sip on that for a few minutes and consider how Liam was answering the questions. He had answered no to every letter. Maybe his last name was still readable on his headstone. The cemetery is hard to go through. The weeds are tall and a large cherry tree lies on the ground in the center of the graves. If I could avoid tramping through all of that, I would feel much better. Then I had an idea.

"Liam, do you know your letters?"

"No."

"Did you learn how to read and write?"

"No."

"Is that why you don't know what letter your name starts with?"

"Yes." The rods quivered just a bit.

"Liam, I'm going to talk to some of the other spirits that are here in the house. Is that okay with you?"

"Yes."

"Daniel, are you here?"

"Yes."

"Did you know Liam when you were alive?"

"No."

"Adelaide, did you know Liam when you were alive?"

"No."

"Did you know about him?"

"Yes."

"Was Liam less intelligent than other people?"

"Yes."

"Did people call him an idiot?" I used the word "idiot" in my questioning because in the 1700s that was the name that people would have used and understood.

"Yes."

"Was he good-hearted?"

"Yes."

Then I went back to Liam to finish my interview.

"Liam, was it hard to learn things?"

"Yes."

"Did people call you names?"

"Yes."

I felt sad for Liam. Perhaps in his new reincarnated life he will have more opportunity to learn and enjoy what he could not enjoy in his last life.

"I hope that when you are reborn that you have a better life. And thank you for talking to me."

With that I ended the interview.

Interview with Pete

This interview took many twists and turns. "Maybe I'm getting tired of talking to dead people," I thought to myself before I started to write down the interview. "Oh well." I sighed deeply and went on.

"Pete, I have started to write a book. Other spirits in the house are going to be considered one of my chapters. Would you be willing to also have a chapter in the book?"

The rods opened wide. "Yes."

"I would like to know when you lived. Was it in the 1900s, 1800s, 1700s, or the 1600s?" Finally I got a yes. This was the oldest spirit in the house. I had never talked to an older spirit than Pete. I was truly excited.

"Pete, have you been in this house since it was built?"

"No."

"Did you, as a spirit, move into the house in the 1900s?"

"Yes."

I was surprised. I was fully expecting to have to go century by century backward to get the answer. "Do you feel comfortable here?"

"Yes."

"I would like to know more about your past. Have you had other lives?"

"Yes." It turned out that Pete had had four lives.

"I would like to know when your soul first entered into a human being. Was it before Christ?"

"No."

"Was it before 100 AD?"

"Yes."

Then I went through the continents. "Did you live in North America, South America, Europe, Asia, and finally Africa?"

"Yes." It was Africa.

"Were you a black man?"

"No."

"An Arab?"

"No"

Okay, who was he? "Were you an Egyptian?" They were a bountiful people back then.

"No."

Now I was doing one of my sitting and pondering sessions. Hmm.

"Were you Jewish?"

The rods made an attempt to open up but wavered a little back and forth.

"Were you Hebrew?"

"Yes." A definite wide separation of the rods occurred.

"Have you always been Hebrew?"

"No."

"Were you a Christian in the 1600s?"

"Yes."

"You have had four lives, so as you earlier said to me, you have something to atone for."

"Yes."

I thought, "I'm not going to kid around and ask a lot of questions about what he did. I'm going for the jugular."

"Did you murder somebody?"

"Yes."

"Was this as Pete?"

"Yes."

"Was it a relative?"

"Yes."

I went through the list of closest relatives and was getting a bit concerned until I came to cousin.

"A cousin?"

"Yes."

"How old were you when you did this? In your twenties?"

"No."

"Your teens?"

"Yes."

"Did you ever get caught?"

"No."

"Did anyone else pay for your crime?"

"No."

"Thank God for that," I said to myself. "Did you ever kill anyone in another life that you lived?" I asked.

"Yes."

"More than twice?"

"Yes."

"Three times?"

"Yes."

"Were you ever a bad man, one that robbed and we would call a villain?"

"Yes."

"Can you point to where you were buried?"

He pointed to the old cemetery.

"Were you buried there?"

"No."

"In the fields beyond the cemetery?"

"No."

I spent about five minutes trying to locate the burial place he was pointing to. Finally we ended up in the town of Groton by the shore. "I would like to know your last name. Is that okay with you?"

"Yes."

I started going through the alphabet and ended up on L. The next letter turned out to be an E. "Is your last name Ledyard?"

"Yes."

I ask him this repeatedly. The answer, yes, was always the same.

That is a famous name in Southeastern Connecticut and I have no proof that his statement was correct.

"Do you think that you could end up in hell?"

"No."

"Is there a hell and have you ever heard of hell fire and brimstone?"

"No."

"So will you keep getting reborn until you get it right or do something so bad that your soul dies with you?"

"Yes."

Interview with the Victim

I sat at my desk so that I could be as still as possible, elbows on desk, knuckles together and relaxed.

"Hello. Is there anyone here?"

The rods opened wide.

"Are you a female?"

"Yes."

"Did you live in this house?"

"Yes."

"Did you die in this house?"

"Yes."

"Did you die of natural causes? Were you sick?"

"No."

"Did you live with your family or a family member?"

"Yes."

"Were you abused by a family member?"

"No."

"Were you left alone a lot?"

"Yes."

"Did a family member kill you?"

"Yes."

"Were you an old lady?"

"Yes."

"Were you murdered in bed?"

"Yes."

"Were you smothered?"

"Yes."

"Are you here so that someone will find out about the way you died?"

"Yes."

"When I bought this home, there was a spirit that I was afraid of. Is that the spirit that murdered you?"

"No."

"Do you know of the spirit that I was afraid of?"

"Yes."

"Is he gone?"

"Yes."

"Is the spirit that murdered you still in this house?"

"No."

"'Thank God,' I say to myself. "Can you go to the light now that someone knows what happened to you?" I asked.

"Yes."

"Will you?"

"No."

"Someday?"

"Yes."

To Write to the Author

If you wish to contact the author or would like more information about this book, please write to to us at The Connecticut Press. Both the author and the publisher appreciate hearing from you and learning of your enjoyment of this book and how it has helped you. While we cannot guarantee that every letter written to us can be answered, all will be forwarded to the author. Please write to:

Carol Matsumoto
℅ The Connecticut Press
63 West Wharf Road
Madison, CT 06443

Please enclose a self-addressed stamped envelope for reply,
or $1.00 to cover costs. If outside the U.S.A., enclose
an international postal reply coupon.

Many of our authors have websites with additional information and resources. For more information, please visit our website at https://www.connecticutpress.com

www.ingramcontent.com/pod-product-compliance
Lightning Source LLC
Chambersburg PA
CBHW070543010526
44118CB00012B/1198